The Ten Con

The Decalogue, Christianity, and the Beast

What do the Ten Commandments mean?

Are Christians supposed to keep the Ten Commandments?

Were the Ten Commandments in place before Mt. Sinai?

Did Jesus endorse or end the Ten Commandments?

Were the Ten Commandments 'nailed to the cross'?

Did Early Gentile Christians keep the Ten Commandments?

What is the Mystery of Iniquity?

Any ties between the Mark of the Beast and the Ten Commandments?

Copyright © 2017 by *Nazarene Books*. ISBN 978-1-940482-92-7. Draft Edition. Booklet produced for the *Continuing* Church of God and Successor, a corporation sole. 1036 W. Grand Avenue, Grover Beach, California, 93433 USA.

Cover photo: The papyrus on the left is from a collection of four papyri fragments acquired in Egypt by W. L. Nash and first described by Stanley A. Cook in 1903. It dates from the second century B.C. The tablet to its right is the oldest found version of most of the Ten Commandments in stone. It is called the Samaritan Decalogue and was carved between 300-500 A.D. Back cover illustration was done by C. Winston Tay for the old Radio Church of God and copyrighted in 1960 and not renewed, hence it is public domain.

Various translations of the Bible are used throughout this text; where no name nor abbreviation is given, then the New King James Version (NKJV) is being cited (Thomas Nelson, Copyright © 1997; used by permission).

CONTENTS

Introduction

Billions of people have heard of the Ten Commandments. There have been court battles related to them and even the display of them.

Even movies have been made related to them. Part of Cecil B. DeMille's 1923 silent film *The Ten Commandments* was filmed in the sand dunes very close to where I am writing this. Yet, that does not make this a highly religious area.

Many claim to try to keep the Ten Commandments, but few really do. Many religion leaders have either claimed that they are 'done away,' changed, or do not really need to be kept as they were intended.

Are the Ten Commandments relevant in the 21st century?

Growing up in a Roman Catholic household, I was aware of the Ten Commandments. In catechism classes, I recall needing to memorize the version that the Church of Rome claimed it believed.

But I really did not know what the Ten Commandments meant until after I studied the Bible more, plus read Church of God literature related to them.

While people realize that the Ten Commandments were written on stone at Mount Sinai and given to Moses, few seem to realize the Bible shows they were established in the beginning. Some believe that Christians have no need to keep the Ten Commandments and claim they were "nailed to the cross."

Are the Ten Commandments a bunch of harsh rules or do they show love and teach God's people how to live?

This is something you need to know.

In the Beginning

"In the beginning, God created the heavens and the earth" (Genesis 1:1). These functioned according to laws of physics that God created. God also made various life forms that functioned according various laws of biology that He made to work with His creation.

God made humans and breathed life into Adam (Genesis 2:7). One way humans differ from animals is because of the "spirit in man" and "the breath

3

of the Almighty" that gives humans understanding (Job 32:8).

There are laws for humans that God decreed so that humans could live better (Deuteronomy 30:19-20). The Bible teaches that "God is love" (1 John 4:8,16) and Jesus said that the God's laws were based on love (Matthew 22:37-40).

The Ten Commandments were first made known to Adam in the Garden of Eden.

How do we know that?

Because the Bible teaches: "through one man sin entered the world" (Romans 5:12)—and that man was Adam (Romans 5:14).

So, what is sin according to Protestant and Catholic translations of the Bible?

> [4] Whosoever committeth sin transgresseth also the law: for sin is the transgression of the law. (1 John 3:4, KJV)

> [4] Whosoever committeth sin commmitteth also iniquity; and sin is iniquity. (1 John 3:4, DRB)

Consider that Romans 5:14 teaches, "death reigned from Adam to Moses."

In Romans 5:13 we read that, "Sin is not imputed when there is no law." Yet sin was imputed, because death did reign from Adam to Moses. There must then have been some law from Adam's time for Adam to have sinned.

The reality is that God's commandments were in effect from the beginning.

It was sin to transgress God's commandments between the time of Adam and Moses. Therefore, the Ten Commandments did not originate at Mount Sinai with Moses.

Consider also the following:

> [13] You were in Eden, the garden of God; Every precious stone was your covering: The sardius, topaz, and diamond, Beryl, onyx, and jasper, Sapphire, turquoise, and emerald with gold. The workmanship of your timbrels and pipes Was prepared for you on the day you were created. (Ezekiel 28:13, NKJV)

¹⁴ Thou a cherub stretched out, and protecting, and I set thee in the holy mountain of God, thou hast walked in the midst of the stones of fire. ¹⁵ Thou wast perfect in thy ways from the day of thy creation, until iniquity was found in thee. (Ezekiel 28:14-15, DRB)

That "cherub" with iniquity was the one who is known as Satan the devil (Revelation 12:9; 20:2). Satan sinned BEFORE Adam and Eve were created. 'Iniquity' existed before Mt. Sinai. God destroyed people in the Great Flood of Noah's time for their wickedness (Genesis 6:6). Since the "wicked man … is caught in the cords of his sin" (Proverbs 5:22), sin (and hence the Ten Commandments existed prior to Mt. Sinai).

How do We Know there are Ten Commandments?

How do we know that there are TEN Commandments?

The commandments are literally called the "ten words" in Exodus 34:28, Deuteronomy 4:13, and Deuteronomy 10:4—and that is how we know there are ten.

The Hebrew terms for the Ten Commandments are literally translated as the "ten words," which is where the term "Decalogue" in English come from (via Greek).

They are called "commandments" in other parts of the Old Testament (e.g. Exodus 20:6) as well as in the New Testament, from Hebrew and Greek words more literally meaning "commandments," but without the numeric designation of ten.

Kept by Gentile Christians

Early church history clearly shows that all real as well as many professing Christians believed that they needed to keep the Ten Commandments.

While some point to the Jerusalem council in Acts 15 as 'proof' that Gentile Christians did not need to keep the Ten Commandments, Christians afterwards did teach that they still needed to be kept.

This is confirmed by writings of early Gentile church leaders such as Polycarp of Smyrna (ordained by the original Apostles), Melito of Sardis, and Theophilus of Antioch who all taught that Christians were to keep the Ten Commandments.

It was only apostates who had some connection to Simon Magus (Acts 8:9-24), like Marcion of Pontus, who taught they were done away. This Marcion was denounced by Polycarp, who "turned away" some of those Marcion deceived "to the Church of God" (Irenaeus. Against Heresies. Book III, Chapter 3, Verse 4).

While some in modern times believe that they know better, those who actually used *koine* Greek (the language of the New Testament) and lived in the first and second centuries obviously better understood the Greek as well as what the Apostles meant.

Early Christians, Jew and Gentile, believed that they were to keep the Ten Commandments. Do not be deceived by clever, false, arguments of men (cf. 2 Peter 2:3, NLT).

The Ten Commandments Show Love

God's commandments show love:

> [2] By this we know that we love the children of God, when we love God and keep His commandments. [3] For this is the love of God, that we keep His commandments. And His commandments are not burdensome. (1 John 5:2-3)

> [6] This is love, that we walk according to His commandments. This is the commandment, that as you have heard from the beginning, you should walk in it. (2 John 6)

The commandments show love and are not a burden for real Christians. Loving your neighbor is part of the royal law, which is a law of liberty:

> [8] If you really fulfill the royal law according to the Scripture, "You shall love your neighbor as yourself," you do well ...[12] So speak and so do as those who will be judged by the law of liberty. (James 2:8, 12)

Christians are to keep the commandments as they will be judged by them.

The First Commandment

Should human life be focused on the physical?

Certainly, most in the world live like life should be.

Oh yes, they have their religious rituals and traditions. And many pray.

But when it comes down to it, God is not what is really important to them.

Yet for Christians, that is not to be the case. Jesus said:

> [31] "Therefore do not worry, saying, 'What shall we eat?' or 'What shall we drink?' or 'What shall we wear?' [32] For after all these things the Gentiles seek. For your heavenly Father knows that you need all these things. [33] But seek first the kingdom of God and His righteousness, and all these things shall be added to you. (Matthew 6:31-33)

Do you put God first?

Decades ago, I remember someone telling me that God should not get in the way of my career. He claimed to be Christian of some type. He obviously did not believe in seeking first the Kingdom of God. But Christians should.

Here is the first commandment from the Book of Exodus:

> [2] "I am the Lord your God, who brought you out of the land of Egypt, out of the house of bondage. [3] "You shall have no other gods before Me. (Exodus 20:2-3)

Because of the reference to God bringing the children of Israel out of Egypt, various ones have concluded that this command, as well as others, was only for the children of Israel.

However, that view overlooks the fact that versions of this command were in place before there were children of Israel as well as after Jesus was resurrected. It also overlooks the fact that the Bible also speaks of spiritual Egypt (Revelation 11:8).

Furthermore, consider whether or not you have ever really come out from the false ways and traditions of this world and have also truly repented of your own lusts and sins. We all must come out of spiritual Egypt.

Notice some of what God said to Abraham:

> ⁷ I am the Lord, who brought you out of Ur of the Chaldeans (Genesis 15:7).

> ¹ I am Almighty God; walk before Me and be blameless. (Genesis 17:1)

The Bible also says:

> ⁵ Abraham obeyed My voice and kept My charge, My commandments, My statutes, and My laws. (Genesis 26:5)

The same Hebrew word translated as 'commandments' here, *mitswotaay*, is also mentioned in Exodus 20:6 when the Ten Commandments were listed.

The passage in Genesis shows that not only did Abraham obey, he knew what God expected. And this was centuries before the Ten Commandments were given at Mount Sinai.

Christians, too, are admonished to be obedient (1 Peter 1:13-14).

What About Adam and Eve?

God is the One we are supposed to obey (Acts 5:32).

Do you realize that's one of the definitions of God?

Whoever you obey most is your god. Whatever you serve could be your god. It might be your automobile. Maybe it's an idol. Maybe it's your boss or family. Whatever it is, that's your god if you obey it and disobey the God of the Bible (cf. Acts 5:29).

> ¹⁶ Do you not know that to whom you present yourselves slaves to obey, you are that one's slaves whom you obey, whether of sin leading to death, or of obedience leading to righteousness? (Romans 6:16)

Adam and Eve had another god in place of the true God. Adam and Eve violated the first commandment. Eve heeded the voice of the serpent (Genesis 3:13) and Adam heeded Eve (Genesis 3:17).

The Greatest Commandment

What is the greatest commandment? Jesus was asked about that:

> [35] Then one of them, a lawyer, asked Him a question, testing Him, and saying, [36] "Teacher, which is the great commandment in the law?"
>
> [37] Jesus said to him, "'You shall love the Lord your God with all your heart, with all your soul, and with all your mind. (Matthew 22:35-37)

Many people say that they love God, but God is not truly real to them. They put other priorities above obeying God.

Consider the following that Joshua stated:

> [14] "Now therefore, fear the Lord, serve Him in sincerity and in truth, and put away the gods which your fathers served on the other side of the River and in Egypt. Serve the Lord! [15] And if it seems evil to you to serve the Lord, choose for yourselves this day whom you will serve, whether the gods which your fathers served that were on the other side of the River, or the gods of the Amorites, in whose land you dwell. But as for me and my house, we will serve the Lord." (Joshua 24:14-15)

Do any Christians really believe that they should serve false gods?

Yet, even though Jesus referred to the first commandment as the greatest commandment, this is the commandment that is violated the most.

The Bible teaches:

> [5] Trust in the Lord with all your heart, And lean not on your own understanding; [6] In all your ways acknowledge Him, And He shall direct your paths. (Proverbs 3:5-6)

However, most will not do that. Instead, most are wise in their own eyes and tend to trust themselves. The Bible warns:

> ⁷ Do not be wise in your own eyes; Fear the Lord and depart from evil. (Proverbs 3:7)

Those that are wise in their own eyes and not properly trusting God are violating the first commandment.

Christians are to pray that GOD's will be done (Matthew 6:10) and have Jesus' attitude of "not My will, but Yours, be done" (Luke 22:42).

As was the case in Jesus' time, many accept 'traditions of men' which nullify their commitment to the commandments of God (cf. Matthew 15:3-9) and will not risk being put out of their compromised churches because "they loved the praise of men more than the praise of God" (John 12:43).

If people actually would keep the first commandment, there would be no more crime. No illegitimate births. No sexually transmitted diseases. No murders. No thefts. Politicians would tell the truth. The world would be a much better place.

The first commandment is that important, and actually more important than that. Its obedience would result in vast abundance and peace. Society would change and spiritual peace would reign.

While Satan would still try to influence people in this age (Ephesians 2:2), people would follow the admonition of James:

> ⁷ Therefore submit to God. Resist the devil and he will flee from you. ⁸ Draw near to God and He will draw near to you. (James 4:7-8)

The world would be a so much better place if people would heed the first commandment.

Why Love God?

Why should you love God? Well:

[17] Every good gift and every perfect gift is from above, and comes down from the Father of lights, with whom there is no variation or shadow of turning. [18] Of His own will He brought us forth by the word of truth, that we might be a kind of firstfruits of His creatures. (James 1:17-18)

Every good gift is from God. Furthermore, Jesus was "the firstborn among many brethren" (Romans 8:29). God has a plan for us to glorify us as He glorified Jesus (cf. John 17:22).

God plans to put the universe under subjection of His resurrected children (Hebrews 2:5-10)!

Additionally, consider:

> [9] We love Him because He first loved us. (1 John 4:19)

> [8] But God demonstrates His own love toward us, in that while we were still sinners, Christ died for us. [9] Much more then, having now been justified by His blood, we shall be saved from wrath through Him. (Romans 5:8-9)

Despite the problems you may have, you have great promises:

> [28] And we know that all things work together for good to those who love God, to those who are the called according to His purpose. (Romans 8:28)

> [6] ... He who has begun a good work in you will complete it until the day of Jesus Christ; (Philippians 1:6)

God made us. All good gifts come from God. Despite our sins, He sent Jesus to die for us (John 3:16). If we love God all things will work out for our good, and thus, God will be faithful until the day of Jesus and glorify us. We have a lot to love God for!

False Confidence

We are to look to the God of the Bible. Yet, many throughout history have turned to astrology, witchcraft, and spiritists instead (Isaiah 47:13-15). That is not something that God's people should do:

> [19] And take heed, lest you lift your eyes to heaven, and when you see the sun, the moon, and the stars, all the host of heaven, you feel driven to worship them and serve them, which the Lord your God has given to all the peoples under the whole heaven as a heritage. (Deuteronomy 4:19)

> [10] There shall not be found among you anyone who makes his son or his daughter pass through the fire, or one who practices witchcraft, or a soothsayer, or one who interprets omens, or a sorcerer, [11] or one who conjures spells, or a medium, or a spiritist, or one who calls up the dead. [12] For all who do these things are an abomination to the Lord, and because of these abominations the Lord your God drives them out from before you. [13] You shall be blameless before the Lord your God. 14 For these nations which you will dispossess listened to soothsayers and diviners; but as for you, the Lord your God has not appointed such for you. (Deuteronomy 18:10-14)

Christians do not read horoscopes, etc. We look to the Bible (Isaiah 8:10; 66:5). Christians do "not follow cunningly devised fables" (2 Peter 1:16).

First Commandment Before Sinai, from Jesus, and After Jesus' Death

The Bible shows the first commandment was in place before Mt. Sinai:

> "I am the LORD, who brought you out of Ur" (Genesis 15:7); "I am Almighty God, walk before me and be blameless" (Gen 17:1); "I am the God of your father--the God of Abraham, the God of Isaac, and the God of Jacob" (Exodus 3:6). "Put away the foreign gods that are among you, purify yourselves" (Genesis 35:2). "and against all the gods of Egypt I will execute judgment: I am the LORD" (Exodus 12:12). "Now I know that the LORD is greater than all the gods; for in the very thing in which they behaved proudly, He was above them" (Exodus 18:11). "This also would be an iniquity deserving of judgement, for I would have denied God who is above" (Job 31:28). "Then Job answered the LORD and said, 'I know that you can do everything, And that no purpose of Yours can be withheld from you'" (Job 42:1-2).

Jesus taught and expanded the first commandment:

> "You shall worship the LORD your God, and Him only you shall serve" (Matthew 4:10). "You shall love the LORD your God with all your heart, with all your soul, and with all your mind. This is the first and the great commandment" (Matthew 22:37). "And you shall love the LORD your God with all your heart, with all your soul, with all your mind, and with all your strength. This is the first commandment" (Mark 12:30). "You shall worship the LORD your God, and Him only you shall serve" (Luke 4:8).

After Jesus was resurrected, the New Testament taught the first commandment:

> Paul said, "God, who made the world and everything in it...they should seek the Lord" (Acts 17:24,27). Paul also said, "I worship the God of my fathers, believing all things which are written in the Law" (Acts 24:14). "And what agreement has the temple of God have with idols?" (2 Corinthians 6:16). "you turned to God from idols to serve the living and true God" (1 Thessalonians 1:9). "Let no one deceive you by any means; for that Day will not come unless the falling away comes first, and the man of sin is revealed, the son of perdition, who opposes and exalts himself above all that is called God or that is worshiped, so he sits as God in the temple of God, showing himself that he is God" (2 Thessalonians 2:3-4). "Do not love the world or the things in the world. If anyone loves the world, the love of the Father is not in him" (1 John 2:15); which is another way of saying, put nothing in the world before God. "If anyone worships the beast and his image, and receives his mark on his forehead or on his hand, he himself shall also drink of the wine of the wrath of God" (Revelation 14:9-10). "Then I saw the souls of those who had been beheaded for their witness to Jesus and for the word of God, who had not worshiped the beast or his image" (Revelation 20:4). "But the...unbelieving...shall have their part in the lake which burns with fire and brimstone, which is the second death" (Revelation 21:8).

The first commandment is not only the most important one, it is the one that is most commonly violated.

Jesus expanded the understanding of this commandment by stating that truly loving God is the greatest of the commandments.

It is wrong to rebel against God by violating the first commandment:

> [22] Has the Lord as great delight in burnt offerings and sacrifices,
> As in obeying the voice of the Lord?
> Behold, to obey is better than sacrifice,
> And to heed than the fat of rams.
> [23] For rebellion is as the sin of witchcraft,
> And stubbornness is as iniquity and idolatry. (1 Samuel 15:22-23)

God expects His people to obey Him.

We should love our Creator and heavenly Father. The first commandment is a reminder to do so.

Seek first the kingdom of God and His righteousness (Matthew 6:33)—put your trust in God (Proverbs 3:5-6) and strive to keep the first commandment.

The Second Commandment

Humans, apart from God, are truly carnally minded:

> [5] For those who live according to the flesh set their minds on the things of the flesh, but those who live according to the Spirit, the things of the Spirit. [6] For to be carnally minded is death, but to be spiritually minded is life and peace. [7] Because the carnal mind is enmity against God; for it is not subject to the law of God, nor indeed can be. [8] So then, those who are in the flesh cannot please God. (Romans 8:5-8)

Yet, the carnally-minded think that they can please God through the veneration of idols and icons.

The carnal mind wants something to help worship God, like something physical to remind Him of the invisible God. This type of item is forbidden in the second commandment.

The second commandment from the Book of Exodus states:

> [4] "You shall not make for yourself a carved image — any likeness of anything that is in heaven above, or that is in the earth beneath, or that is in the water under the earth; [5] you shall not bow down to them nor serve them. For I, the Lord your God, am a jealous God, visiting the iniquity of the fathers upon the children to the third and fourth generations of those who hate Me, [6] but showing mercy to thousands, to those who love Me and keep My commandments. (Exodus 20:4-6)

Jesus warned:

> [22] You worship what you do not know; we know what we worship, for salvation is of the Jews. [23] But the hour is coming, and now is, when the true worshipers will worship the Father in spirit and truth; for the Father is seeking such to worship Him. [24] God is Spirit, and those who worship Him must worship in spirit and truth. (John 4:22-24)

People accept idols, icons, and traditions as superior to the word of God and then do not worship God in truth. God only wants people to worship Him in spirit and in truth!

Those who really know the true Creator God as his Father do not need a picture or icon to assist with prayer. One who believes otherwise has not come to know God — and is not filled with and led by the Spirit of God. In order to worship God in spirit, you must have His Holy Spirit. "Now if anyone does not have the Spirit of Christ, he is not His" (Romans 8:9).

God only gives His Holy Spirit after repentance and baptism — and only to those who OBEY Him (Acts 2:38; 5:32).

Consider the following from the New Jerusalem Bible (a Catholic translation):

> [4] Draw me out of the net they have spread for me, for you are my refuge; [5] to your hands I commit my spirit, by you have I been redeemed. God of truth, [6] you hate those who serve useless idols; but my trust is in Yahweh: (Psalm 31:4-6. NJB)

The God of truth hates worship with idols.

Now, you may tell yourself that your veneration of the cross, saints, etc. is the religion of your ancestors and hence is acceptable. But that is wrong.

Melito of Sardis ran into similar arguments in the second century:

> How can the unseen God be sculptured? Nay, it is the likeness of thyself that thou makest and worshippest. Because the wood has been sculptured, hast thou not the insight to perceive that it is still wood, or that the stone is still stone? The gold also the workman: taketh according to its weight in the balance. And when thou hast had it made into an image, why dose thou weigh it? Therefore thou art a lover of gold, and not a lover of God...
>
> Again, there are persons who say: Whatsoever our fathers have bequeathed to us, that we reverence. Therefore, of course, it is, that those whose fathers have bequeathed them poverty strive to become rich! and those whose fathers did not instruct them, desire to be instructed, and to learn that which their fathers knew not! And why, forsooth, do the children of the blind see, and the children of the lame

walk? Nay, it is not well for a man to follow his predecessors, if they be those whose course was evil; but rather that we should turn from that path of theirs, lest that which befell our predecessors should bring disaster upon us also...

And then shall those who have not known God, and those who have made them idols, bemoan themselves, when they shall see those idols of theirs being burnt up, together with themselves, and nothing shall be found to help them. (Melito. A Discourse Which Was in the Presence of Antoninus Caesar)

While many people consider Melito to be a saint, many ignore his warning against idols and tradition. Jesus warned against putting traditions above God's commandments (Matthew 15:3-9) and putting family considerations above following Him (Matthew 10:37).

Many supposedly 'Christian' symbols are from idolatrous paganism. Many people combine pagan worship practices, which the Apostle Paul warns about as follows:

[19] What am I saying then? That an idol is anything, or what is offered to idols is anything? [20] Rather, that the things which the Gentiles sacrifice they sacrifice to demons and not to God, and I do not want you to have fellowship with demons. 21 You cannot drink the cup of the Lord and the cup of demons; you cannot partake of the Lord's table and of the table of demons. (1 Corinthians 10:19-22)

Christians should keep God's Holy Days and not observe compromised pagan substitutes (for more information on this, please check out our booklet *Should You Observe God's Holy Days or Demonic Holidays?*).

The Bible teaches that God made humankind in His image (Genesis 1:27). Yet, it also teaches against humans making figures of God in according to their image or imagination or seeing physical objects (Deuteronomy 4:15-19).

It may be of interest to note that many of the most commonly used pictures of Jesus are actually believed to have originally been an attempt to make Jesus look like a younger version of Zeus (Taylor J. What did Jesus really look like? BBC, December 24, 2015).

Christians are to "walk by faith, not by sight" (2 Corinthians 5:7), yet like the pagans of old, many are excessively awed by colorful images (Ezekiel 23:14-16; 1 Kings 12:28-31) and stubbornly cling to various forms of idolatry (cf. 1 Samuel 15:23).

Modern Idols?

Now, you may not bow down before crosses, deities, or saints. But could you be making your job, social status, money, appetite, or possessions your idol?

Many people do.

People will worship modern idols by covetously seeking possessions, status, money, or many such things.

Notice that this is truly is a form of idolatry:

> [5] Therefore put to death your members which are on the earth: fornication, uncleanness, passion, evil desire, and covetousness, which is idolatry. (Colossians 3:5, NKJV)

> [5] So put to death the sinful, earthly things lurking within you. Have nothing to do with sexual immorality, impurity, lust, and evil desires. Don't be greedy, for a greedy person is an idolater, worshiping the things of this world. (Colossians 3:5. NLT)

There is a reason that the Bible warns:

> [10] For the love of money is a root of all kinds of evil, for which some have strayed from the faith in their greediness, and pierced themselves through with many sorrows. (1 Timothy 6:10)

Money, of itself, is not evil—but breaking the commandments is.

Loving the physical above God is a modern type of idolatry.

Consider also the following:

[16] Now behold, one came and said to Him, "Good Teacher, what good thing shall I do that I may have eternal life?"

[17] So He said to him, "Why do you call Me good? No one is good but One, that is, God. But if you want to enter into life, keep the commandments."

[18] He said to Him, "Which ones?"

Jesus said, "'You shall not murder,' 'You shall not commit adultery,' 'You shall not steal,' 'You shall not bear false witness,' [19] 'Honor your father and your mother,' and, 'You shall love your neighbor as yourself.'"

[20] The young man said to Him, "All these things I have kept from my youth. What do I still lack?"

[21] Jesus said to him, "If you want to be perfect, go, sell what you have and give to the poor, and you will have treasure in heaven; and come, follow Me."

[22] But when the young man heard that saying, he went away sorrowful, for he had great possessions. (Matthew 19:16-22)

The young man thought he kept the Ten Commandments, but his attachment to the physical showed he did not "seek first the kingdom of God" (Matthew 6:33) and was guilty of covetous idolatry.

It is not that holding possessions has to be a problem (Abraham, Isaac, Jacob, and King David were all wealthy), but this man may have had an opportunity to be an apostle or hold some other leadership role. Yet, let his possessions get in his way.

Do your possessions get in the way?

While you may not think you are as important as a king or ancient patriarch, "it is better to be a doorkeeper in the house of My God" (Psalm 84:10) than to make an idol of your possessions (cf. Luke 12:15).

Some will work on the Sabbath and/or Holy Days because they idolize their job or paycheck.

Some will not give tithes and/or sufficient offerings because of their attachment to them and their lack of faith in the true God.

Consider that Jesus said:

> [20] Fool! [21] ... is he who lays up treasure for himself, and is not rich toward God." (Luke 12:20-21)

Although God's plan does include repentant idolaters (cf. Isaiah 42:16-18) venerating statues/icons or coveting possessions is idolatry and is not being rich towards God.

As cited earlier, 1 Samuel 15:22-23 teaches that stubbornness is as idolatry. In Deuteronomy 21:20, the Bible ties gluttony and being a drunkard in with stubbornness. Be careful that your eating and drinking practices are not a form of idolatry.

Second Commandment Before Sinai, from Jesus, and After Jesus' Death

The Bible shows the second commandment was in place before Mt. Sinai:

> "'Put away the foreign gods that are among you, purify yourselves'...So they gave Jacob all the foreign gods which were in their hands, and the earrings which were in their ears and Jacob hid them" (Genesis 35:2,4). "And you shall not let any of your descendants pass through the fire of Molech ... for all these abominations the men of the land have done, who were before you, and thus the land is defiled" (Leviticus 18:21,27). "If I have observed the sun when it shines, or the moon moving in its brightness, so that my heart has been secretly enticed, and my mouth has kissed my hand; This also would be an iniquity deserving of judgement, For I would have denied God who is above" (Job 31:26-28) (note this is believed to be part of idol worship).

Jesus taught and expanded the second commandment:

"You shall worship the LORD your God, and Him only you shall serve" (Matthew 4:10). "You shall worship the LORD your God, and Him only you shall serve" (Luke 4:8). "God is spirit, and those who worship Him must worship in spirit and truth" (John 4:24). "But I have a few things against you, because you have there those who hold the doctrine of Balaam...to eat things sacrificed to idols" (Revelation 2:14). "Nevertheless, I have a few things against you, because you allow...My servants to...eat things sacrificed to idols" (Revelation 2:20).

After Jesus was resurrected, the New Testament taught the second commandment:

"we write to them to abstain from things polluted by idols" (Acts 15:20). "Now while Paul waited for them in Athens, his spirit was provoked within him when he saw that the city was given over to idols...Then Paul stood in the midst of the Areopagus and said...'God, who made the world and everything in it, since He is Lord of heaven and earth, does not dwell in temples made with hands. Nor is He worshipped with men's hands, as though He needed anything'" (Acts 17:16,22,24-25). "Professing to be wise, they became fools, and changed the glory of the incorruptible God into an image made like corruptible man--and birds and four footed animals and creeping things" (Romans 1:22-23). "But now I have written to you not to keep company with anyone named a brother, who is...an idolater" (1 Corinthians 5:11). "Neither... idolators...will inherit the kingdom of God" (1 Corinthians 6:9-10). "And do not become idolaters as were some of them...Therefore, my beloved, flee from idolatry" (1 Corinthians 10:7,14). "And what agreement has the temple of God have with idols?" (2 Corinthians 6:16). "Now the works of the flesh are evident...idolatry" (Galatians 5:19,20). "For this you know that no ... idolater, has any inheritance in the kingdom of Christ and God" (Ephesians 5:5). "Therefore put to death...covetousness, which is idolatry" (Colossians 3:5). "you turned to God from idols" (1 Thessalonians 1:9). "abominable idolatries" (1 Peter 4:3). "Little children, keep yourselves from idols" (1 John 5:21). "But I have a few things against you, because you have there those who hold the doctrine of Balaam...to eat things sacrificed to idols" (Revelation 2:14). "Nevertheless, I have a few things against you, because you allow...My servants to...eat things sacrificed to idols" (Revelation 2:20). "But the

21

rest of mankind, who were not killed by these plagues, did not repent of the works of their hands, that they should not worship demons, and idols of gold, silver, brass, stone, and wood, which can neither see nor hear nor walk" (Revelation 9:20). "But ...idolaters...shall have their part in the lake which burns with fire and brimstone, which is the second death" (Revelation 21:8). "But outside are...idolaters" (Revelation 22:15).

While the New Testament does not explicitly state not to bow down to graven images, it does teach that idolatry is wrong and that covetousness is a form of idolatry.

Furthermore, the New Testament expands on the second commandment by explaining that it also includes covetousness and that God only wants to be worshiped in truth. No idol or icon is true to God nor should be bowed before.

The Third Commandment

Do words matter?

Certainly.

Jesus taught:

> [37] For by your words you will be justified, and by your words you will be condemned. (Matthew 12:37)

The United States has long been the world leader in producing movies. Yet, because some believe that those having a 'G' (General Audience) rating could harm their marketing efforts, vulgar language is often included in movies.

Such things should not be done (cf. 1 Timothy 6:9-10).

The Apostle Paul wrote:

> [8] But now you yourselves are to put off all these: anger, wrath, malice, blasphemy, filthy language out of your mouth. (Colossians 3:8-9)

So, we see that the New Testament prohibits both blasphemy, which is speaking improperly about God, as well as filthy language, which can also include speaking against God.

Christians are admonished to:

> [29] Let no corrupt word proceed out of your mouth, but what is good for necessary edification, that it may impart grace to the hearers. (Ephesians 4:29)

So, more than just not taking God's name in vain, Christians are to speak that which is good.

The third commandment from the Book of Exodus states:

[7] "You shall not take the name of the Lord your God in vain, for the Lord will not hold him guiltless who takes His name in vain. (Exodus 20:7)

We need to be careful about using God's name. Many claim that God has done this or that for them, when He has not. Various ones claim many things are God's will, even their bad choices, when that is not the will of God.

Because "holy and reverend is his {God's} name" (Psalms 111:9, KJV), we do not refer to ministers or others as with titles like "reverend." And because Jesus said, "Do not call anyone on earth your father; for One is your Father, He who is in heaven" (Matthew 23:9), we do not refer to religious leaders as "father" (that title is basically reserved for our physical fathers and our Father in heaven).

Please also consider that those who are not truly Christians are taking God's name in vain if they call themselves Christians.

(It should be noted that blasphemy against the Holy Spirit—Matthew 12:31-32 and Hebrews 6:4-6–involves turning against the truth by the truly converted as well as the ways of God, and is not a result of inadvertently cursing.)

What About 'Sacred Names'?

Some believe that it is wrong for Christians to use terms like God, Jesus, or Lord. They believe that this is using God's name in vain.

Typically, because of what is called the 'tetragrammaton,' YHVH (translated as 'LORD' or 'Lord' in many Protestant and Catholic Bibles), these people believe that the Father must be called Jehovah, Yahveh, or Yahweh. They normally prefer some version of the term Yeshua to refer to Jesus.

While it can be proper to use terms like Yahveh or Yeshua, many fail to realize that the New Testament was basically written in Greek. Though some claim that the New Testament was originally written in Hebrew or Aramaic, scholars have concluded that the Greek New Testament does NOT show signs of being translated (other than obviously various statements of Jesus made in Aramaic, etc.).

The reality is that the inspired New Testament does use words properly translated into English as God, Jesus, or Lord.

Ignoring what language the New Testament was originally written in, when Jesus was dying and He prayed, He did NOT refer to His Father as Yahveh or Yahweh:

> ⁴⁶ And about the ninth hour Jesus cried out with a loud voice, saying, "Eli, Eli, lama sabachthani?" that is, "My God, My God, why have You forsaken Me?" (Matthew 27:46)

Notice that the biblical translation was that Jesus was calling out to God. In the entire New Testament, Jesus is NEVER quoted using any of the "sacred names" that many claim is necessary.

This clearly demonstrates that Jesus did NOT feel He had to refer to God the Father as any 'sacred name.' While Christians are to be respectful, it is not biblically correct to insist on 'sacred names.'

Furthermore, since there are no vowels in ancient Hebrew, no one is 100% certain as to how various names in the Old Testament were pronounced. And in the New Testament Greek, Jesus' name is not Y'eshua—it is closer to *Ieesou*.

It should also be understood that Jesus told His followers to refer to His Father as Father when praying (Matthew 6:9)—not any version of YHVH.

The New Testament most certainly DOES NOT require sacred names, and not using them is NOT a violation of the third commandment.

Euphemistically Using God's Name in Vain

Satan has influenced society (Ephesians 2:2) and many people curse using God's name in vain.

Satan has deceived the whole world (Revelation 12:9). Many believe that they can say versions of these curses with semi-substitutes.

Various ones vainly make statements like, "Oh, my God!" when they are not praying to God, but others will use similar statements, like, "Oh, my gosh!" or

"Oh, my goodness!" which is a euphemistic way to say the same thing. On the internet, "OMG" is also used a lot. Such should not be done.

Many, when upset, scream, "Jesus!," again not in prayer. Others, do the same basic thing when they cry out, "Geez!"

There are also other improper statements.

Do not euphemistically use God's name in vain. Do not call yourself Christian if you will not be willing to live as Jesus wanted you to (cf. 1 Corinthians 11:1; 1 John 2:6).

Perhaps it should be mentioned that the reason we in the *Continuing* Church of God do not say, "God bless you" after someone sneezes is because that tradition is based on the unbiblical notion that an evil spirit may enter someone who sneezes and must be warded off with some type of a spell. If someone is truly ill they can pray and others can also pray for them (James 5:13-14).

Third Commandment Before Sinai, from Jesus, and After Jesus' Death

The Bible shows the third commandment was in place before Mt. Sinai:

> "nor shall you profane the name of your God...for all these abominations the men of the land have done, who were before you, and thus the land is defiled" (Leviticus 18:21,27). "It may be that my sons have sinned and cursed God in their hearts" (Job 1:5). "Curse God and die!" (Job 2:9). Interestingly, those called of God are not to be cursed either, "And I will curse him who curses you" (Genesis 12:3).

Jesus taught and expanded the third commandment:

> "pray: Our Father in heaven, Hallowed be Your name" (Matthew 6:9). "Therefore I say to you, every sin and blasphemy will be forgiven men, but the blasphemy against the Spirit will not be forgiven men" (Matthew 12:31). "For out of the heart proceed evil thoughts, ...blasphemies. These are the things which defile a man" (Matthew 15:19-20). "What comes out of a man, that defiles a man. 21 For from

26

within, out of the heart of men, proceed evil thoughts ... blasphemy, pride, foolishness" (Mark 7:20-22).

After Jesus was resurrected, the New Testament taught the third commandment:

"they are all under sin...Whose mouth is full of cursing and bitterness" (Romans 3:9,14). "Let all...evil speaking be put away from you" (Ephesians 4:31). "But now you yourselves are to put off all these:...blasphemy, filthy language out of your mouth" (Colossians 3:8). "they may learn not to blaspheme" (1 Timothy 1:20). But know this, that in the last days perilous times will come: For men will be...blasphemers" (2 Timothy 3:1,2). "Out of the same mouth proceed blessing and cursing. My brethren, these things ought not to be so" (James 3:10). "He is the antichrist who denies the Father and the Son" (1 John 2:22).

Do not take God's name in vain.

The Fourth Commandment

Our lives are often busy.

We need to become educated, make a living, take care of our families, etc. There are also numerous distractions and various ones who want to impose on our time.

Do humans need a rest from the world of today?

The Book of Genesis teaches the following:

> [1] Thus the heavens and the earth, and all the host of them, were finished. [2] And on the seventh day God ended His work which He had done, and He rested on the seventh day from all His work which He had done. [3] Then God blessed the seventh day and sanctified it, because in it He rested from all His work which God had created and made. (Genesis 2:1-3)

Who did Jesus say God made the Sabbath for?

> [27] "The Sabbath was made for man, and not man for the Sabbath. [28] Therefore the Son of Man is also Lord of the Sabbath." (Mark 2:27-28)

Some, including those calling themselves Jehovah's Witnesses, have claimed that God made the Sabbath for Himself in Genesis 2 and that He then gave it to the Jews over 2500 years later.

But Jesus said the Sabbath was made for man, meaning all humans and not just Jews. Furthermore, although many want to call Sunday 'The Lord's Day,' in the Bible, Jesus said He was Lord of the Sabbath.

In the English language, the seventh-day of the week is called Saturday. Yet, most who profess Christianity either do not believe it needs to be kept at all or believe to some degree it is to be kept on Sunday.

But the Bible never teaches that.

The fourth commandment from the Book of Exodus is listed as follows:

> [8] "Remember the Sabbath day, to keep it holy. [9] Six days you shall labor and do all your work, [10] but the seventh day is the Sabbath of the Lord your God. In it you shall do no work: you, nor your son, nor your daughter, nor your male servant, nor your female servant, nor your cattle, nor your stranger who is within your gates. [11] For in six days the Lord made the heavens and the earth, the sea, and all that is in them, and rested the seventh day. Therefore the Lord blessed the Sabbath day and hallowed it. (Exodus 20:8-11)

People should work when they need to and rest on the Sabbath. This author has long considered the Sabbath to be a paid vacation. It is paid by working throughout the week, and since it is a command of God, one can be confident that God will provide when you take that one day per week off.

Christians are to Observe the Seventh Day Sabbath

Many oppose the Sabbath. Some have even argued that the New Testament does not enjoin the seventh-day Sabbath, but that is an erroneous belief.

Jesus taught:

> [4] "It is written, 'Man shall not live by bread alone, but by every word that proceeds from the mouth of God.'" (Matthew 4:4)

The Apostle Paul taught:

> [16] All Scripture is given by inspiration of God, and is profitable for doctrine, for reproof, for correction, for instruction in righteousness, [17] that the man of God may be complete, thoroughly equipped for every good work. (2 Timothy 3:16-17)

So, does the portion of scripture known as the New Testament enjoin keeping the Sabbath for Christians?

Notice what the New Testament Book of Hebrews teaches using two Protestant and three Catholic translations:

[3] Now we who have believed enter that rest, just as God has said, "So I declared on oath in my anger, 'They shall never enter my rest.'" And yet his work has been finished since the creation of the world. [4] For somewhere he has spoken about the seventh day in these words: "And on the seventh day God rested from all his work." [5] And again in the passage above he says, "They shall never enter my rest." [6] It still remains that some will enter that rest, and those who formerly had the gospel preached to them did not go in, because of their disobedience...[9] There remains, then, a Sabbath-rest for the people of God; [10] for anyone who enters God's rest also rests from his own work, just as God did from his. [11] Let us, therefore, make every effort to enter that rest, so that no one will fall by following their example of disobedience (Hebrews 4:3-6,9-11, NIV).

[3] For we who have believed enter that rest, just as He has said, "AS I SWORE IN MY WRATH, THEY SHALL NOT ENTER MY REST," although His works were finished from the foundation of the world. [4] For He has said somewhere concerning the seventh day: "AND GOD RESTED ON THE SEVENTH DAY FROM ALL HIS WORKS"; [5] and again in this passage, "THEY SHALL NOT ENTER MY REST." [6] Therefore, since it remains for some to enter it, and those who formerly had good news preached to them failed to enter because of disobedience,.. [9] So there remains a Sabbath rest for the people of God. [10] For the one who has entered His rest has himself also rested from his works, as God did from His. [11] Therefore let us be diligent to enter that rest, so that no one will fall, through following the same example of disobedience. (Hebrews 4:3-6,9-11, NASB)

[3] We, however, who have faith, are entering a place of rest, as in the text: And then in my anger I swore that they would never enter my place of rest. Now God's work was all finished at the beginning of the world; [4] as one text says, referring to the seventh day: And God rested on the seventh day after all the work he had been doing. [5] And, again, the passage above says: They will never reach my place of rest. [6] It remains the case, then, that there would be some people who would reach it, and since those who first heard the good news were prevented from entering by their refusal to believe...[9] There must still be, therefore, a seventh-day rest reserved for God's people, [10] since to enter the place of rest is to rest after your work, as God did after

his. ¹¹ Let us, then, press forward to enter this place of rest, or some of you might copy this example of refusal to believe and be lost. (Hebrews 4:3-6,9-11, NJB)

³ For we, that have believed, shall enter into their rest; as he said: As I sware in my wrath, if they shall enter into my rest: and truly the works from the foundation of the world being perfected. ⁴ For he said in a certain place of the seventh day thus: And God rested the seventh day from all his works...⁹ Therefore there is left a sabbatisme for the people of God. ¹⁰ For he that is entered into his rest, the same also hath rested from his works, as God did from his. ¹¹ Let us hasten therefore to enter into that rest; lest any man fall into the same example of incredulity. (Hebrews 4:3-6,9-11, The Original and True Rheims New Testament of Anno Domini 1582)

3 For we who believed enter into [that] rest, just as he has said: "As I swore in my wrath, 'They shall not enter into my rest,'" and yet his works were accomplished at the foundation of the world. 4For he has spoken somewhere about the seventh day in this manner, "And God rested on the seventh day from all his works"; 5 and again, in the previously mentioned place, "They shall not enter into my rest." 6 Therefore, since it remains that some will enter into it, and those who formerly received the good news did not enter because of disobedience,... 9 Therefore, a sabbath rest still remains for the people of God. 10And whoever enters into God's rest, rests from his own works as God did from his. 11 Therefore, let us strive to enter into that rest, so that no one may fall after the same example of disobedience. (Hebrews 4:3-6,9-11, New American Bible)

Thus, this clearly shows that the command to keep the seventh day Sabbath is in the New Testament. The New Testament also shows that only those who will not observe it because of their disobedience argue otherwise. Early Christians realized that the Sabbath was in place for God's people.

Even Origen of Alexandria understood some of this as he wrote:

But what is the feast of the Sabbath except that which the apostle speaks, "There remaineth therefore a Sabbatism," that is, the observance of the Sabbath, by the people of God...let us see how the Sabbath ought to be observed by a Christian. On the Sabbath-day all worldly labors ought to be abstained from...give yourselves up to spiritual exercises, repairing to church, attending to sacred reading and instruction...this is the observance of the Christian Sabbath (Translated from Origen's Opera 2, Paris, 1733, Andrews J.N. in History of the Sabbath, 3rd edition, 1887, pp. 324-325).

One reason that many today do not understand this is that certain translators have intentionally mistranslated the Greek term *sabbatismos* (ςαββατισμός) which is actually found in Hebrews 4:9 (Green JP. The Interlinear Bible, 2nd edition. Hendrickson Publishers, 1986, p. 930).

The Protestant KJV and NKJV mistranslate it, as does the CHANGED version of the Rheims New Testament, also known as the Challoner version (changed in the 18th century). All three of them mistranslate the word as 'rest.'

Yet, there is a different Greek term (*katapausin*), translated as 'rest' in the New Testament. *Sabbatismos* clearly refers to a 'sabbath-rest' and honest scholars will all admit that. Because of the mistranslations, most today do not realize that the seventh-day Sabbath was specifically enjoined for Christians in the New Testament.

If you are Roman Catholic, consider the following:

Codex Amiatinus The most celebrated manuscript of the Latin vulgate Bible, remarkable as the best witness to the true text of St. Jerome... (Fenlon, John Francis. "Codex Amiatinus." The Catholic Encyclopedia. Vol. 4. New York: Robert Appleton Company, 1908)

Here is the Latin from the *Codex Amiatinus*:

9 itaque relinquitur sabbatismus populo Dei (Hebrews 4:9, *Codex Amiatinus*)

It should be clear, even to non-Latin readers, that Hebrews 4:9 is definitely talking about the Sabbath.

Decades ago, a Protestant told this author that the reason he did not keep the seventh-day Sabbath was because it was not taught for Christians in the New Testament. So, he was handed an RSV Bible and told to read Hebrews 4. After doing so, he said because his grandmother was a "good Christian" in his view, and because she did not keep it, he felt that he should not. He failed to truly rely on the Bible, but instead relied on false tradition (cf. Mark 7:6-8). Sadly most who profess Christianity do not keep the seventh-day Sabbath and rely mainly on improper traditions, whether they realize it or not.

Notice something from the Jehovah's Witness's translation of scripture:

> [9] So there remains a sabbath-rest for the people of God. (Hebrews 4:9, NWT, 2013)

So, the Jehovah's Witnesses should know the truth about this commandment as well—but they also do not keep the Sabbath.

For those interested in another source, here is a translation of Hebrews 4:9 from the, *Eastern Peschitta*, which is an Aramaic text (Roth AG, Daniel BB. Aramaic English New Testament, 5th edition. Netazari Press, 2012):

> [9.] For there remains a Shabat for the people of Elohim.

Here is a claimed translation from a 'Hebrew' New Testament (which some call the Brit HaHadashah):

> [9] There remaineth therefore a sabbath rest for the people of God.

Whether we look at translations from the Greek, the early Latin Vulgate, Aramaic, or Hebrew, it should be clear that the Bible does enjoin Sabbath-keeping for Christians.

Although the Sabbath is a time of refreshing rest, many ignore that and consider it a burden. Notice the following prophecy that seems to apply to those who do not keep the Sabbath:

> [11] For with stammering lips and another tongue He will speak to this people, [12] To whom He said, "This is the rest with which You may cause

the weary to rest," And, "This is the refreshing"; Yet they would not hear. (Isaiah 28:11-12)

Will you hear?

The seventh-day Sabbath remains for the true people of God.

Keeping the Sabbath

Keeping the Sabbath shows and builds faith. One trusts that God will provide if one is honoring God and truly keeping His commandments.

The Sabbath is kept from sunset on the day commonly called Friday through sunset on the day commonly called Saturday.

It is kept by doing the work we need to for six days (Exodus 20:9; cf. 2 Thessalonians 3:1-12) and then resting on the seventh (Exodus 20:10).

Christians should pray, mediate, and study the word of God on the Sabbath. Part of how we rest on the Sabbath is not going to our jobs or secular classes then nor doing carnal work nor classwork then.

Christians are to meet with, and encourage, others (Hebrew 10:24-25). The Sabbath is to be a holy convocation (Leviticus 23:2), which means that we attend church services if possible (we do not attend if we are ill and may infect others).

Because of distance, if one cannot attend with others, church services can be done alone with watching appropriate sermon and sermonette videos, etc. (the weekly *Letter to the Brethren* of the *Continuing* Church of God has a suggested Sabbath service format for scattered individuals who have internet access).

While one should not spend the entire Sabbath discussing carnal matters, and there are various matters that should not be discussed until after the Sabbath is over, one does not need to limit all conversions to only spiritual matters.

Notice the following:

¹³ "If you turn away your foot from the Sabbath,
From doing your pleasure on My holy day,
And call the Sabbath a delight,
The holy day of the Lord honorable,
And shall honor Him, not doing your own ways,
Nor finding your own pleasure,
Nor speaking your own words,
¹⁴ Then you shall delight yourself in the Lord;
And I will cause you to ride on the high hills of the earth,
And feed you with the heritage of Jacob your father.
The mouth of the Lord has spoken." (Isaiah 58:13-14)

The Sabbath is to be called a delight. Yet, many who profess Christ call it an *unnecessary burden.*

Christians are spiritually Israelites (cf. Romans 2:28-29; Revelation 3:7-9) and heirs to the promises (Galatians 3:9). So, notice that the promises to Israel (Jacob) can be ours if we properly keep God's Sabbath, His Holy Day.

We are not to pursue carnal pursuits on the Sabbath (cf. Isaiah 58:13). Hence, we do not engage in sports, watch worldly entertainment, go shopping (though there could be an emergency), engage in physical exercise, etc. on the Sabbath. However, that does not mean one cannot take a walk or appreciate aspects of God's creation on the Sabbath.

Some have been confused about cooking. Cooking can be done on the Sabbath, as can bathing/showering. The commands against kindling a fire in the Old Testament (Exodus 35:3) had to do with industrial fires and not cooking:

> **Ye shall kindle no fire throughout your habitations upon the sabbath day**. The Sabbath was not a fast day. The Israelites cooked their victuals on that day, for which, of course, a fire would be necessary; and this view of the institution is supported by the conduct of our Lord (Luke 14:1) ... As the kindling of a fire, therefore, could only be for secular purposes (Jamieson, Fausset, and Brown Commentary).

So, cooking and food preparation can be appropriate (cf. Exodus 12:6). But one should not work oneself hard to cook on the Sabbath. Keep the Sabbath day holy.

Jesus also said that traveling can affect food acquisition on the Sabbath (Mark 2:23-26), and we will often eat out then if we are out-of-town.

Jesus taught that we are to do good on the Sabbath (Matthew 12:12).

While it is needful to take care of children and livestock (Luke 13:15) on the Sabbath, just because it may be the "busy season" at work does not mean that a Christian should violate the Sabbath to do carnal work (Exodus 34:21).

While Jesus said the work of God can be done on the Sabbath (cf. Matthew 12:5), this does not mean normal physical work. Though certain emergency situations can be handled (Luke 14:4). Yet, one should prepare for the Sabbath and reduce the possibility of such 'emergencies.'

Family Matters and Pleasures

As far as children go, this author and his wife have raised three, one of whom still lives with us. The other two, who have moved out of the house, still keep the Sabbath.

We would teach them, throughout the week, but more about the Bible on the Sabbath. We tried to instruct them as God commands (Deuteronomy 6:6-7).

We also tried to not make the Sabbath an unnecessarily difficult burden for them. But that also does not mean that we were particularly liberal with our rules either.

Unlike some parents, we did not take them to restaurants on the Sabbath (unless we were traveling), did not allow them (or ourselves) to watch television for entertainment, nor did we allow them to play secular video games.

We did, however, allow them to play Bible-based video games, which tended to be more like quizzes. That is probably one of the reasons that our oldest son ended up developing various games/quizzes that are linked to the cogwriter.com website.

We did sometimes have livestock and we would tend to share the tasks of feeding and/or milking on the Sabbath (we never had more than one or two goats to milk). We would also tend to share other tasks that might have been needful on the Sabbath, such as meal preparation. But not massively time-consuming/complicated meal preparation, but also not intentionally plain meals either.

Of course, as we did not shop on the Sabbath, go to school on the Sabbath, nor go to work on the Sabbath, neither did our children.

It should also be noted that we all have some (or a lot of) formal education, and never did we do school-work or attend classes on the Sabbath. It is not that it was always easy, but the point is to state that it can be done--although in cultures with required or nearly required attendance on the Sabbath, this can be a much more difficult challenge, but there are also others who report that they successfully were able to handle this.

We also did allow our children, when young, to sometimes play outside with friends. We also would sometimes take our children to a park and sometimes take them to the beach. We tried to keep the Sabbath as a pleasant and holy day. Unlike some children brought up in various Church of God groups, our children did NOT dread the coming of the Sabbath nor do we (author and his wife) recall our children ever complaining about keeping the Sabbath.

As far as adults go, since this subject has come up before, based upon various scriptures (e.g. 1 Corinthians 7:3-4), marital relations are not forbidden on the Sabbath.

All people should attend services on the Sabbath, with others when possible:

> [24] And let us consider one another in order to stir up love and good works, [25] not forsaking the assembling of ourselves together, as is the manner of some, but exhorting one another, and so much the more as you see the Day approaching. (Hebrews 10:24-25)

Christians are not to just focus on themselves, but should exhort other Christians as we get closer to the return of Jesus and the establishment of the millennial kingdom of God.

The Sabbath helps picture the millennial reign. Because of statements, various scriptures, Jews (Psalm 90:4; Psalm 92) and early Christians (2 Peter 3:8; Hebrews 4:6-8; Revelation 20:4-6) believed that the Sabbath helped picture the millennium. Essentially, they taught that the six days of physical creation represented six one-thousand year days, followed by the Sabbath, representing the millennial rest. Jewish tradition also seemingly attributes statements by Elijah confirming this (Babylonian Talmud: Sanhedrin 97a).

Even Greco-Roman-Protestant saint Irenaeus realized this as he wrote:

> These are [to take place] in the times of the kingdom, that is, upon the seventh day, which has been sanctified, in which God rested from all the works which He created, which is the true Sabbath of the righteous, which they shall not be engaged in any earthly occupation; but shall have a table at hand prepared for them by God, supplying them with all sorts of dishes (Against Heresies. Book V, Chapter 33, Verse 2)

So did the 4th century Greco-Roman saint and bishop Methodius:

> For I also, taking my journey, and going forth from the Egypt of this life, came first to the resurrection, which is the true Feast of the Tabernacles, and there having set up my tabernacle, adorned with the fruits of virtue, on the first day of the resurrection, which is the day of judgment, celebrate with Christ the millennium of rest, which is called the seventh day, even the true Sabbath. (Methodius. Banquet of the Ten Virgins, Discourse 9, chapter 5)

Jerome observed that 5th century Sabbath-keeping Christians also believed that the seven-day Feast of Tabernacles also pictured the millennium (Jerome, Commentariorum in Zachariam Lib. III. Patrologia Latina 25, 1529; 1536). One interesting aspect of this is that the Bible teaches that the Book of Deuteronomy is to be read every seven years during the Feast of Tabernacles (Deuteronomy 31:10-13), and that includes reading the version of the Ten Commandments listed in its 5th chapter.

The Bible teaches that the millennial reign will be a fantastic time and that the law will be taught then (Isaiah 2:2-4; Micah 4:1-4) with reminders given by God's teachers to observe it (Isaiah 30:20-21).

The Sabbath is a weekly reminder that God's millennial kingdom will come.

In this current age, the Sabbath is to be a blessing:

> [1] Thus says the Lord:
>
> "Keep justice, and do righteousness,
> For My salvation is about to come,
> And My righteousness to be revealed.
> [2] Blessed is the man who does this,
> And the son of man who lays hold on it;
> Who keeps from defiling the Sabbath,
> And keeps his hand from doing any evil." (Isaiah 56:1-2)

The Bible teaches that ALL of God's "commandments are righteousness" (Psalm 119:172), and that obviously includes the Sabbath as Isaiah 56:1-2 points out.

The righteous keep the Sabbath.

Fourth Commandment Before Sinai, from Jesus, and After Jesus' Death

The Bible shows the fourth commandment was in place before Mt. Sinai:

> "And on the seventh day God ended His work which He had done, and He rested on the seventh day from all His work which He had done. Then God blessed the seventh day and sanctified it, because in it He rested from all His work which God had created and made" (Genesis 2:2-3). "Is there not a time of hard service for man on the earth" (Job 7:1). "the triumping of the wicked is short...Because he knows no quietness in his heart" (Job 20:5,20). "Tomorrow is a Sabbath rest, a holy Sabbath to the LORD ... How long do you refuse to keep My commandments and My laws? See! For the Lord has given you the

Sabbath ... So the people rested on the seventh day" (Exodus 16:23, 28-30). "The Sabbath was made for man" (Mark 2:27).

Jesus taught and expanded the fourth commandment:

"What man is there among you who has one sheep, and it falls into a pit on the Sabbath, will not lay hold of it and lift it out? Of how much more value then is a man than a sheep? Therefore, it is lawful to do good on the Sabbath" (Matthew 12:11-12). "And pray that your flight may not be in winter or on the Sabbath" (Matthew 24:20); there would be no reason to pray this if the Sabbath was not going to be in existence. "And He said to them, 'The Sabbath was made for man, and not man for the Sabbath. Therefore the Son of Man is also Lord of the Sabbath'" (Mark 2:27); this verse tells all who will see which day is the Lord's Day. "And when the Sabbath had come, He began to teach in the synagogue" (Mark 6:2). "And as His custom was, He went into the synagogue on the Sabbath day, and stood up to read" (Luke 4:16). "Then He went down to Capernaum, a city of Galilee, and was teaching them on the Sabbaths" (Luke 4:31). "The Son of Man is also Lord of the Sabbath...Is it lawful on the Sabbath to do good or to do evil, to save life or to destroy?" (Luke 6:5,9). "But the ruler of the synagogue answered with indignation, because Jesus had healed on the Sabbath...The Lord then answered him and said, 'Hypocrite...So ought not this woman...be loosed from this bond on the Sabbath?'" (Luke 13:14-16). "'Is it lawful to heal on the Sabbath?'...And they could not answer Him regarding these things" (Luke 14:3,6). "are you angry with Me because I made a man completely well on the Sabbath?" (John 7:23).

Jesus did not "do away with the Sabbath." Jesus eliminated extra "traditions" that the Pharisees added to the Sabbath commandment. He emphasized that the Sabbath was for doing good.

Jesus never taught that the Sabbath was supposed to be on Sunday.

After Jesus was resurrected, the New Testament taught the fourth commandment:

"Then Paul, as his custom was, went in to them and for three Sabbaths reasoned with them from the Scriptures...And he reasoned in the synagogue every Sabbath, and persuaded both Jews and Greeks" (Acts 17:2;18:4 see also 13:14,27,42,44). "let him labor, working with his hands what is good, that he may have something to give to him who has need" (Ephesians 4:28) and "For even when we were with you, we commanded you this: 'If anyone will not work, neither shall he eat'" (2 Thessalonians 3:10); (recall that the requirement to work is also part of the Sabbath command, thus even that portion of the commandment is repeated in the New Testament.) "And to whom did He swear they would not enter His rest, but to those who did not obey?" (Hebrews 3:18). "For He has spoken in a certain place of the seventh day in this way: 'And God rested on the seventh day from all His works'" (Hebrews 4:4). "There remains therefore a rest (literally *sabbatismos*, 'Sabbath rest') for the people of God. For he who has entered His rest has himself also ceased from his works as God did from His" (Hebrews 4:9-10). That day was the Preparation and the Sabbath drew near...And they rested on the Sabbath in accordance with the commandment" (Luke 23:54,56). "But when they departed from Perga, they came to Antioch in Pisidia, and went into the synagogue on the Sabbath day and sat down" (Acts 13:14), they seemed to be following this admonition from John, "He who says he abides in Him ought also to walk just as He walked" (I John 2:6), since Jesus always went to the synagogues on the Sabbath (Luke 4:16), Christians are to keep the Sabbath.

No one in the New Testament is shown teaching that Sunday was the replacement for Saturday.

The late Roman Catholic Cardinal James Gibbons wrote:

You may read the Bible from Genesis to Revelation, and you will not find a single line authorizing the sanctification of Sunday. The Scriptures enforce the religious observance of Saturday, a day which we never sanctify. (Gibbons J., Cardinal. The faith of our fathers: being a plain exposition and vindication of the church founded by Our Lord Jesus Chris, 83rd reprint edition. P.J. Kenedy, 1917, pp. 72-73)

The seventh-day Sabbath, and not Sunday, is the day of rest in the Bible, and even Catholic leaders know this.

Those willing to "live by ... every word that proceeds from the mouth of God" (Matthew 4:4) keep the seventh-day Sabbath.

The Fifth Commandment

When Adam and Eve sinned, they also dishonored their only parent.

In the New Testament Adam is called the "son of God" (Luke 3:38). This is because God created him. Adam was the son of God by a direct creation. Adam was not God's son by regular human begettal or birth. Eve, was fashioned by God out of Adam's rib (Genesis 2:21-23), and hence was not born the usual way.

Adam not only dishonored God, but he also broke the tenth commandment. There was also lust when the woman saw that it was good for food and desired to make one wise; vanity, egotism and pride entered into her heart (Genesis 3:6) which would violate the ninth commandment. She put the word of the serpent over the word of God and hence violated the first commandment. She made an idol out of worldly wisdom (cf. 1 Corinthians 3:19) and thus violated the second commandment.

Lust is what usually causes a person to have an inordinate desire to have something that is not to be theirs. Lust can cause some to steal, and Adam and Eve broke the eighth commandment by stealing what was not theirs to take.

At least six of the Ten Commandments were broken when Eve partook of the forbidden fruit.

And in other ways every one of the Ten Commandments was actually broken in that first human sin. Improperly disobeying parents can lead to many problems.

The fifth commandment, from the Book of Exodus, states:

> [12] "Honor your father and your mother, that your days may be long upon the land which the Lord your God is giving you. (Exodus 20:12)

The version in Deuteronomy is a bit longer:

> [16] 'Honor your father and your mother, as the Lord your God has commanded you, that your days may be long, and that it may be well

with you in the land which the Lord your God is giving you. (Deuteronomy 5:16)

Deuteronomy means 'second law' and all the Ten Commandments are repeated in the 5th chapter of Deuteronomy.

If children would honor their parents and parents were honorable, it would go well in the physical land.

A disobedient child is a frustrated child as that child's mind is often plagued with feelings of guilt and rebellion. Children who love, honor, and obey their parents are blessed.

In modern times, it is also realized that those who come from more stable families are less likely to be involved in crime.

Children are to Be Taught

Children do not naturally know how to do right and they need to be taught.

One of the biggest 'secrets' of being a successful parent is to spend time with your child(ren).

Those that follow what the Bible teaches will teach their children. Notice what the Bible shows God said right after Moses reiterated the Ten Commandments in Deuteronomy:

> [6] "And these words which I command you today shall be in your heart. [7] You shall teach them diligently to your children, and shall talk of them when you sit in your house, when you walk by the way, when you lie down, and when you rise up. [8] You shall bind them as a sign on your hand, and they shall be as frontlets between your eyes. [9] You shall write them on the doorposts of your house and on your gates. (Deuteronomy 6:6-9)

> [6] Train up a child in the way he should go, And when he is old he will not depart from it. (Proverbs 22:6).

Children who learn God's words and commands will learn about what is right.

When children have proper boundaries and are taught right from wrong as the Bible teaches, they can avoid many pitfalls in the world. They also will tend to be happier (cf. Psalm 144:15; Proverbs 28:14).

The Bible also teaches:

> [3] Behold, children are a heritage from the Lord, The fruit of the womb is a reward. [4] Like arrows in the hand of a warrior, So are the children of one's youth. [5] Happy is the man who has his quiver full of them; They shall not be ashamed, But shall speak with their enemies in the gate. (Psalm 127:3-5)

Parents should properly correct their children. The Bible teaches:

> [13] Don't fail to discipline your children. They won't die if you spank them. (Proverbs 23:13, New Living Translation, NLT)

> [10] Harsh discipline is for him who forsakes the way, And he who hates correction will die. (Proverbs 15:10)

> [17] Correct your son, and he will give you rest; Yes, he will give delight to your soul. (Proverbs 29:17)

Most children should not need much in the way of "harsh" discipline. And in modern society, be cautious about the wisdom of spanking (legally it is not allowed in various countries). But children should have rules and boundaries and be subject to discipline if they violate those rules and boundaries.

There are many ways to provide discipline to your children. Talking with them, removing or restricting privileges, as well as my favorite, giving children additional work to do. Having children pull weeds was one of this author's favorite forms of disciplinary punishment. Also, as they get older, properly raised children normally will respond to simply expressing your disappointment in them as sufficient discipline.

Consider also that the Bible teaches, "And the hope of the hypocrite shall perish" (Job 8:13)--if you hope that your children will turn out well, then try not to live as a hypocrite. Not being a hypocrite goes a long way in helping parents to be honorable.

Does the fifth commandment mean that children must obey their parents if they are told to violate God's law?

No. "We ought to obey God rather than men" (Acts 5:29). But honorable parents will not tell their children to disobey God's laws.

Are children to obey dishonorable parents in other ways? That depends, but overall children are to honor their parents, whether they are honorable or not. Parents are to act honorably whether their children honor them or not.

Teaching Children Helps Them

The Book of Proverbs repeatedly mentions that it is good for children to listen to their parents:

> [8] My son, hear the instruction of your father, And do not forsake the law of your mother; [9] For they will be a graceful ornament on your head, And chains about your neck. (Proverbs 1:8-9)

> [1] Hear, my children, the instruction of a father, And give attention to know understanding; [2] For I give you good doctrine: Do not forsake my law. [3] When I was my father's son, Tender and the only one in the sight of my mother, [4] He also taught me, and said to me: "Let your heart retain my words; Keep my commands, and live. (Proverbs 4:1-4)

> [20] My son, keep your father's command, And do not forsake the law of your mother. [21] Bind them continually upon your heart; Tie them around your neck. [22] When you roam, they will lead you; When you sleep, they will keep you; And when you awake, they will speak with you. [23] For the commandment is a lamp, And the law a light; Reproofs of instruction are the way of life, [24] To keep you from the evil woman, From the flattering tongue of a seductress. (Proverbs 6:20-24)

The Bible teaches that children should listen to good advice from their parents. Notice also:

¹ Children, obey your parents in the Lord, for this is right. (Ephesians 6:1)

Children are not to obey if parents tell them to violate God's law.

Adult Children

Adult children should be polite to their parents, when possible, whether or not they are particularly honorable.

Proverbs teaches:

> ²⁶ He who mistreats his father and chases away his mother Is a son who causes shame and brings reproach. (Proverbs 19:26)
>
> ²² Listen to your father who begot you, And do not despise your mother when she is old. (Proverbs 23:22)

It is normally advisable for adults to attempt to maintain at least some contact with parents—though this does not mean compromising on holy days or the world's holidays.

In biblical times, adult children were also expected to financially support their parents when they were elderly.

The Pharisees tried to reason around this, but notice what Jesus taught:

> ⁹ He said to them, "All too well you reject the commandment of God, that you may keep your tradition. ¹⁰ For Moses said, 'Honor your father and your mother'; and, 'He who curses father or mother, let him be put to death.' ¹¹ But you say, 'If a man says to his father or mother, "Whatever profit you might have received from me is Corban" — ' (that is, a gift to God), ¹² then you no longer let him do anything for his father or his mother, ¹³ making the word of God of no effect through your tradition which you have handed down. And many such things you do." (Mark 7:9-13)

What about today?

Do adult children have any financial obligations to support their parents?

Yes (cf. 1 Timothy 5:8).

However, in the case of many Western societies, it often is unnecessary. Yet, if it is necessary, adult children still have that obligation.

But what about enabling destructive behavior?

If a parent is a drug-addict, an alcoholic, pornography addict, purposely deceitful, or otherwise is participating in harmful behaviors, should adult children enable this?

No (cf. Galatians 6:1-2; Proverbs 23:20-21; 30:15; 2 Thessalonians 3:10-12; Matthew 18:6). Consider also:

> [11] And have no fellowship with the unfruitful works of darkness, but rather expose them. (Ephesians 5:11)

Hence, while food, clothing, and lodging may need to be provided by adult children, 'cash-money' to a parent who would tend to improperly spend on bad behaviors is not something anyone should give.

Furthermore, while you are to honor your parents, understand that Jesus taught against putting family considerations/traditions above following Him (Matthew 10:37; 15:3-9).

Fifth Commandment Before Sinai, from Jesus, and After Jesus' Death

The Bible shows the fifth commandment was in place before Mt. Sinai:

> "Adam, the son of God" (Luke 3:38), "Because you have heeded the voice of your wife, and eaten from the tree of which I commanded you, saying, 'You shall not eat it of it'": Cursed is the ground for your sake" (Genesis 3:17). "Now therefore, my son, obey my voice" (Genesis 27:43). "Jacob had obeyed his father and his mother" (Genesis 28:7). Notice that later a blessing of land is promised for those who obey this commandment (Exodus 20:12; Deuteronomy 5:16).

Jesus taught and expanded the fifth commandment:

> "For God commanded saying, 'Honor your father and your mother' and 'He who curses father or mother, let him be put to death'" (Matthew 15:4). "Honor your father and your mother" (Matthew 19:19). "Honor your father and your mother" (Mark 7:10). "Honor your father and your mother" (Mark 10:19). "You know the commandments: ... Honor your father and your mother" (Luke 18:20).

After Jesus was resurrected, the New Testament taught the fifth commandment:

> "being filled with all unrighteousness ... disobedient to parents" (Romans 1:29,30). "Children obey your parents in the Lord, for this is right. 'Honor your father and mother', which is the first commandment with promise: that it may be well with you and you may live long on the earth" (Ephesians 6:1-3). "the wrath of God is coming upon the sons of disobedience" (Colossians 3:6). "Children obey your parents in all things, for this is well pleasing to the Lord" (Colossians 3:20). "But know this, that in the last days perilous times will come: For men will be...disobedient to parents" (2 Timothy 3:1,2). "Therefore gird up the loins of your mind, be sober, ... as obedient children" (1 Peter 1:13-14). "They have a heart trained in covetous practices and are accursed children" (2 Peter 2:14). "Behold what manner of love the Father has bestowed upon us, that we should be called children of God" (1 John 3:1).

The world would be a much nicer place if children would honor their parents and the parents made themselves more honorable.

The Sixth Commandment

Imagine a world that is safe.

Around $2 trillion dollars per year is spent on militaries worldwide. Massive amounts are also spent on police forces and security services.

Money that goes towards killing or preventing getting killed could go to aid humankind instead of protect against it.

The first physical murder recorded in the Bible is when Cain killed his brother Abel (Genesis 4:8).

But murder began before there were human beings. Notice what Jesus said:

> [44] You are of your father the devil, and the desires of your father you want to do. He was a murderer from the beginning, and does not stand in the truth, because there is no truth in him. When he speaks a lie, he speaks from his own resources, for he is a liar and the father of it. (John 8:44)

Satan's deceit to Adam and Eve ultimately resulted in their death (cf. Genesis 2:17; 5:5).

The sixth commandment, from the Book of Exodus, states:

> [13] "You shall not murder. (Exodus 20:13)

Yet, most who profess Christianity have reasoned around the truth that command contains.

Military Service and Sports

It is well documented that early Christians would not voluntarily enter the military. Nor would they watch violent sports.

Even most Greco-Romans who professed Christ held to that view until the 4th century, when most accepted the decrees and influence of the follower of the sun-god Mithras, named Constantine.

"Mithraism was first and foremost a military cult" (Aiken CF. Mithraism. The Catholic University bulletin, Volume 19, 1913, p. 255). Emperor Constantine attempted to blend his pagan views with what he considered to be Christianity (Herbermann C, Georg G. Constantine the Great. The Catholic Encyclopedia, 1908).

Many went along with Emperor Constantine.

Even Protestant reformers, including Martin Luther, took militaristic views of Christianity (cf. Luther's Works, vol. Xx, pp. 2230-2632).

Yet, Jesus taught His servants would not fight In this age (John 18:36). in His *Sermon on the Mount*, He taught to be angry against one without cause risked judgment (Matthew 5:22). Because of these teachings and the teaching to "love your neighbor as yourself" (Matthew 22:39), early Christians would not only not join the military, they would not even watch violent sports (cf. Theophilus of Antioch. To Autolycus, Book III, Chapter XV).

Wanting someone to be injured or to somehow be intentionally struck by someone else for entertainment does not show 'Philadelphian love' and should not be encouraged.

Philadelphia means 'brotherly love.' Yet, most who profess Christ do not seem to be bothered by encouraging violence against others.

In the Kingdom of God, "Nation shall not lift up sword against nation, Neither shall they learn war anymore" (Micah 4:3).

Control Your Anger

Jesus warned against improper anger (Matthew 5:22).

Yet some are proud of their tempers. Others blame their anger on their upbringing and/or ethnic origin and are unwilling to change. Although all are affected by their environments, we are not to nurse our anger.

But the Bible says that anger is not to control us in both the Old and New Testaments:

> [4] Be angry, and do not sin. Meditate within your heart on your bed, and be still. (Psalm 4:4)

> [32] He who is slow to anger is better than the mighty, And he who rules his spirit than he who takes a city. (Proverbs 16:32)

> [11] The discretion of a man makes him slow to anger, And his glory is to overlook a transgression. (Proverbs 19:11)

> [9] Do not hasten in your spirit to be angry, For anger rests in the bosom of fools. (Ecclesiastes 7:9)

> [26] "Be angry, and do not sin": do not let the sun go down on your wrath, [27] nor give place to the devil. (Ephesians 4:26-27)

Additionally, notice the following:

> [1] A soft answer turns away wrath, But a harsh word stirs up anger. 2 The tongue of the wise uses knowledge rightly, But the mouth of fools pours forth foolishness. (Proverbs 15:1-2)

> [18] A wrathful man stirs up strife, But he who is slow to anger allays contention. (Proverbs 15:18)

> [16] "Behold, I send you out as sheep in the midst of wolves. Therefore be wise as serpents and harmless as doves. (Matthew 10:16)

Not only are we not to be improperly angry, it is wise for God's people to help others who may be angry towards us if we can.

We are also to pray for them:

> [44] But I say to you, love your enemies, bless those who curse you, do good to those who hate you, and pray for those who spitefully use you and persecute you, [45] that you may be sons of your Father in heaven;

for He makes His sun rise on the evil and on the good, and sends rain on the just and on the unjust. [46] For if you love those who love you, what reward have you? Do not even the tax collectors do the same? [47] And if you greet your brethren only, what do you do more than others? Do not even the tax collectors do so? [48] Therefore you shall be perfect, just as your Father in heaven is perfect. (Matthew 5:44-48)

Jesus set a standard above merely not murdering. We are to love and pray for our enemies and strive for perfection!

Sixth Commandment Before Sinai, from Jesus, and After Jesus' Death

The Bible shows the sixth commandment was in place before Mt. Sinai:

"You are of your father the devil, and the desires of your father you want to do. He was a murderer from the beginning" (John 8:44) (since the devil was a murderer from the beginning it seems clear that murder was not allowed before Mount Sinai). "Cain rose up against Abel his brother and killed him...And He said, 'The voice of your brother's blood cries out to Me from the ground. So now you are cursed from the earth" (Genesis 4:8,11). "Then the king of Egypt spoke ... 'When you do the duties of a midwife for the Hebrew women, and see them on the birthstools, if it is a son, then you shall kill him'...But the midwives feared God, and did not do as the king of Egypt commanded them" (Exodus 1:15-17). "The murderer rises with the light; He kills the poor and needy" (Job 24:14).

Jesus taught and expanded the sixth commandment:

"You have heard that it was said to those of old, 'You shall not murder', and whoever murders will be in danger of the judgment. But I say to you that whoever is angry with his brother without a cause shall be in danger of the judgment" (Matthew 5:21-22). "For out of the heart proceed evil thoughts, murders...These are the things which defile a man" (Matthew 15:19-20). "You shall not murder" (Matthew 19:18). "...murders...All these evil things come from within and defile a man" (Mark 7:21,23). "Do not murder" (Mark 10:19). "You know the commandments:...Do not murder" (Luke 18:20).

53

Even being angry at one improperly is considered by God to be murder.

After Jesus was resurrected, the New Testament taught the sixth commandment:

> "being filled with all unrighteousness...murder" (Romans 1:29). "You shall not murder" (Romans 13:9). "Now the works of the flesh are evident...murders" (Galatians 5:19,21). "the lawless and insubordinate ... murders ... manslayers" (1 Timothy 1:9). "But let none of you suffer as a murderer" (1 Peter 4:15). "For He who said, 'Do not commit adultery,' also said, 'Do not murder'. Now if you do not commit adultery, but you do murder, you have become a transgressor of the law" (James 2:11). "You lust...You murder" (James 4:2)."Whoever hates his brother is a murderer, and we know that no murderer has eternal life abiding in him" (1 John 3:15). "And they did not repent of their murders" (Revelation 9:21). "he who kills with the sword must be killed with the sword" (Revelation 13:10). "But ...murderers...shall have their part in the lake that burns with fire and brimstone, which is the second death" (Revelation 21:8). "But outside are...murderers" (Revelation 22:15).

Notice that unrepentant murderers will not make it. They will not have access to the tree of life (Revelation 22:14).

The Seventh Commandment

Adultery and other forms of sexual immorality are rampant. Many "have eyes full of adultery" (2 Peter 2:14) and like adulterers in the past do not consider adultery nor fornication to be a sin—they think they "have done no wickedness" (Proverbs 30:20).

With the advent of photography in the 19th century, along with movies in the 20th and 21st centuries, and also the internet, there has been a massive rise in the production and viewing of pornography.

Pornography, especially in this internet age, can become addictive. Research shows it distorts one's view of the opposite sex as it often displays people in terms of sexual response (especially women) unrealistically. Pornography can play a role in sexual infidelities as well as in societal sexual crimes such as rape and child molestation. Christians need to flee pornography and all other forms of illicit sexual experimentation (1 Corinthians 6:18; Matthew 5:28).

Satan has managed to get lust and other false sexual messages to spread far and wide. Satan wants YOU to be unfaithful.

Yet, centuries before Mt. Sinai, Israel's son Joseph stated he would not sin by committing adultery (Genesis 39:9). Adultery is also called sin in the New Testament (2 Peter 2:14).

The Bible has many admonitions against adultery, and many passages in the Book of Proverbs provide warnings against it (cf. Proverbs 2:10-20; 5:15-23; 6:23-34; 7:1-27; 23:26-28). They warn that words of an adulteress are deceptive. And of course, any married person involved in adultery has also violated their marriage vows.

The only form of sexual relations that the Bible sanctions is between a male married to a female (cf. Hebrews 13:4; 1 Corinthians 7:3-5). Bestiality (Leviticus 20:15-16), fornication (Galatians 5:19), homosexuality (Leviticus 18:22), incest (Leviticus 18:6-17), prostitution (Deuteronomy 23:17-18), and lesbianism (Romans 1:26) are all condemned.

Fantasy sex is also condemned (Job 31:1,9-11; Matthew 5:28).

Masturbation is either improper lust (1 John 2:16) or else a desire for relief—"but God provided for male, through the means of nocturnal emissions during sleep" (Armstrong HW. Missing Dimension in Sex, 1981) for males, making masturbation always unnecessary. Masturbation also has a variety of undesirable mental and social affects as studies from the old Soviet Union concluded—flee from it (cf. 1 Corinthians 6:18).

The societal cost for fornication, unwed motherhood, divorce, and sexually-transmittal diseases is high and should never be. There would be less broken homes, less juvenile delinquency, and less disease if people would obey the seventh commandment.

The seventh commandment, from the Book of Exodus, states:

> [14] "You shall not commit adultery. (Exodus 20:14)

The sexual and reproductive drives that God made can be quite powerful. This drive was at least partially intended to get many people to look for a spouse (Genesis 2:18; Matthew 19:4-5; Proverbs 18:22, 30:19; 1 Corinthians 7:9) as well as to motivate them to improve their situations so that they could properly raise their own families (cf. Malachi 2:15; Genesis 29:18; 1 Timothy 5:8; Titus 2:3-8). Sexual immorality, such as fornication and masturbation, divert that drive away from God's intended purposes. For young men, it should motivate to take steps to be able to provide for a family (cf. 1 Timothy 5:8). For young women, it should motivate them to be able to properly raise a family (cf. Titus 2:4).

A major point of marriage is love, not lust. Men are to "love your wives, just as Christ also loved the church and gave Himself for her" (Ephesians 5:25). Women are to "to love their husbands, to love their children" (Titus 2:4.) But adultery is a hurtful "lust of the flesh" (cf. Galatians 5:16,19) and not love.

Consider also:

> [14] Do not be unequally yoked together with unbelievers. For what fellowship has righteousness with lawlessness? And what communion has light with darkness? [15] And what accord has Christ with Belial? Or what part has a believer with an unbeliever? (2 Corinthians 6:14-15)

A real Christian should not marry one who is not a real Christian nor incorporate paganism into worship practices.

There are clearly spiritual ramifications of marriage.

The Apostle Paul also wrote:

> ³¹ "For this reason a man shall leave his father and mother and be joined to his wife, and the two shall become one flesh." ³² This is a great mystery, but I speak concerning Christ and the church. (Ephesians 5:31-32)

So, consider there are not only physical principles involved in the seventh commandment. We are to pursue the truth of God and strive to faithfully be one with God (John 17:11).

Spiritual Adultery

The Bible also specifically teaches against spiritual adultery:

> ⁴ Adulterers and adulteresses! Do you not know that friendship with the world is enmity with God? Whoever therefore wants to be a friend of the world makes himself an enemy of God. (James 4:4)

> ⁶ And the person who turns to mediums and familiar spirits, to prostitute himself with them, I will set My face against that person and cut him off from his people. (Leviticus 20:6)

> ³ ... I found it necessary to write to you exhorting you to contend earnestly for the faith which was once for all delivered to the saints. ⁴ For certain men have crept in unnoticed, who long ago were marked out for this condemnation, ungodly men, who turn the grace of our God into lewdness and deny the only Lord God and our Lord Jesus Christ.

> ⁵ But I want to remind you, though you once knew this, that the Lord, having saved the people out of the land of Egypt, afterward destroyed those who did not believe. ⁶ And the angels who did not keep their

proper domain, but left their own abode, He has reserved in everlasting chains under darkness for the judgment of the great day; 7 as Sodom and Gomorrah, and the cities around them in a similar manner to these, having given themselves over to sexual immorality and gone after strange flesh, are set forth as an example, suffering the vengeance of eternal fire. (Jude 3-7)

The Bible condemns both physical and spiritual adultery, and urges Christians to keep the original faith—a faith which included the observance of the Ten Commandments.

Spiritual adultery includes compromising and adding pagan practices and beliefs to what should be the true faith. This was shown in the New Testament and is also prophesied to be a major problem in the end times (Revelation 17).

The Bible also warns that some who claimed to be Christian would not obey:

12 But these, like natural brute beasts made to be caught and destroyed, speak evil of the things they do not understand, and will utterly perish in their own corruption, 13 and will receive the wages of unrighteousness, as those who count it pleasure to carouse in the daytime. They are spots and blemishes, carousing in their own deceptions while they feast with you, 14 having eyes full of adultery and that cannot cease from sin, enticing unstable souls. They have a heart trained in covetous practices, and are accursed children. 15 They have forsaken the right way and gone astray, following the way of Balaam the son of Beor, who loved the wages of unrighteousness; 16 but he was rebuked for his iniquity: a dumb donkey speaking with a man's voice restrained the madness of the prophet.

17 These are wells without water, clouds carried by a tempest, for whom is reserved the blackness of darkness forever.

18 For when they speak great swelling words of emptiness, they allure through the lusts of the flesh, through lewdness, the ones who have actually escaped from those who live in error. 19 While they promise them liberty, they themselves are slaves of corruption; for by whom a person is overcome, by him also he is brought into bondage. (2 Peter 2:12-19)

Those who teach 'liberty' from the Ten Commandments are really bringing people into "bondage of corruption" (Romans 8:21).

Avoid Potentially Compromising Situations

The Apostle Paul warned:

> [18] Flee sexual immorality. Every sin that a man does is outside the body, but he who commits sexual immorality sins against his own body. (1 Corinthians 6:18)

One does not flee sexual immorality by seeing how close one can get to it.

The Book of Proverbs teaches:

> [23] For the commandment is a lamp, And the law a light; Reproofs of instruction are the way of life, [24] To keep you from the evil woman, From the flattering tongue of a seductress. [25] Do not lust after her beauty in your heart, Nor let her allure you with her eyelids. [26] For by means of a harlot A man is reduced to a crust of bread; And an adulteress will prey upon his precious life. [27] Can a man take fire to his bosom, And his clothes not be burned? [28] Can one walk on hot coals, And his feet not be seared? [29] So is he who goes in to his neighbor's wife; Whoever touches her shall not be innocent. (Proverbs 6:23-29)

Consider that Jesus told His followers to pray:

> [13] And do not lead us into temptation, But deliver us from the evil one. (Matthew 6:13)

Nor should Christians lead themselves into temptation. Consider also that the Apostle Paul wrote:

> [22] Abstain from all appearance of evil. (1 Thessalonians 5:22, KJV)

Therefore, married people should not flirt, be involved in sexting, or other improper behaviors with those that are not their spouses. Unmarried people should never be involved with sexting (and this author is not advising married people to actually do this either) and compromising situations.

Avoiding fornication is good for marriage:

> Federal government statistics show that the prospects for an early divorce are minimal among American couples who have never had any sexual partners other than their spouses, and increases with the number of other partners.

> Among couples who have not had other partners, 95% of marriages remain intact through at least the first five years. That number drops to 62% if the woman has had any other partner, and to nearly 50% if she has had two other partners. The numbers also drop, although less sharply, if the man has had other partners. (Statistics show marriages more likely to survive if couples had no other lifetime sexual partners. CNS, 02/13/17).

Society would be so much better off if the seventh commandment were truly kept.

Divorce

The Bible shows that marriage is intended to last a lifetime:

> [10] Now to the married I command, yet not I but the Lord: A wife is not to depart from her husband. [11] But even if she does depart, let her remain unmarried or be reconciled to her husband. And a husband is not to divorce his wife. (1 Corinthians 7:10-11)

> [3] The Pharisees also came to Him, testing Him, and saying to Him, "Is it lawful for a man to divorce his wife for just any reason?"

> [4] And He answered and said to them, "Have you not read that He who made them at the beginning 'made them male and female,' [5] and said, 'For this reason a man shall leave his father and mother and be joined to his wife, and the two shall become one flesh'? [6] So then, they are no longer two but one flesh. Therefore what God has joined together, let not man separate."

7 They said to Him, "Why then did Moses command to give a certificate of divorce, and to put her away?"

8 He said to them, "Moses, because of the hardness of your hearts, permitted you to divorce your wives, but from the beginning it was not so. 9 And I say to you, whoever divorces his wife, except for sexual immorality, and marries another, commits adultery; and whoever marries her who is divorced commits adultery."

10 His disciples said to Him, "If such is the case of the man with his wife, it is better not to marry."

11 But He said to them, "All cannot accept this saying, but only those to whom it has been given: (Matthew 19:3-11).

The disciple saw the limitation Jesus gave as very difficult. It should motivate people to be careful about marriage. While the Bible endorses marriage, nowhere does the Bible teach that marriage will be easy (cf. 1 Corinthians 7:28). It is intended to help build loving character (cf. Ephesians 5:22-33)—and that is not always easy (John 6:33; 1 Corinthians 7:33-34).

Many people will claim something to the effect that their spouse is 'impossible,' not realizing "that all things work together for good to those who love God, to those who are the called according to His purpose" (Romans 8:28) and not having faith that God can work things out. Many do not have enough faith to realize that God knew there would be marital difficulties, but that He expects His people to grow and change through the process. Not having sufficient faith in God, etc. many who profess Christianity trust in themselves (cf. Proverbs 3:6-7) and divorce.

Yet, God hates divorce:

15 But did He not make them one, Having a remnant of the Spirit? And why one? He seeks godly offspring. Therefore take heed to your spirit, And let none deal treacherously with the wife of his youth. 16 "For the Lord God of Israel says That He hates divorce, For it covers one's garment with violence," Says the Lord of hosts. "Therefore take heed to your spirit, That you do not deal treacherously." (Malachi 2:15-16)

There is a very large church that claims to be the original church, yet it allows its priests put away their wives so that they can become 'bishops.' Priests that do that "deal treacherously with the wife of his youth." That and other behaviors God hates.

The Bible also speaks of divorce and remarriage as adultery (Matthew 19:9).

We are to keep our marriage vows (Malachi 2:14), even when it is not easy (cf. Psalm 15:4).

While the Bible mentions a couple of exceptions (cf. Matthew 5:32, 19:9; 1 Corinthians 7:13-15,39), most who have divorced in the eyes of their government and/or church and then remarried are considered to be adulterers by the God of the Bible (cf. Matthew 19:9). They are not learning the way of love as they should.

Seventh Commandment Before Sinai, from Jesus, and After Jesus' Death

The Bible shows the seventh commandment was in place before Mt. Sinai:

> "his master's wife cast longing eyes on Joseph, and she said, 'Lie with me.' But he refused...'How then can I do this great wickedness, and sin against God?'" (Genesis 39:7-9). "Moreover, you shall not lie carnally with your neighbor's wife to defile yourself with her...for all these abominations the men of the land have done, who were before you, and thus the land is defiled" (Leviticus 18:20,27). "The eye of the adulterer waits for the twilight, saying, 'No one will see me'; and he disguises his face" (Job 24:15). Job, a married man, said, "I have made a covenant with my eyes; Why then should I look upon a young woman?" (Job 31:1).

Jesus taught and expanded the seventh commandment:

> "You have heard that it was said to those of old, 'You shall not commit adultery'. But I say to you that whoever looks at a woman to lust for her has already committed adultery with her in his heart" (Matthew 5:27-28). "But I say to you that whoever divorces his wife for any reason except sexual immorality causes her to commit adultery; and

whoever marries a woman who is divorced commits adultery" (Matthew 5:32). "For out of the heart proceed evil thoughts...adulteries, fornications...These are the things which defile a man" (Matthew 15:19-20). "And I say to you, whoever divorces his wife, except for sexual immorality, and marries another, commits adultery, and whoever marries her who is divorced commits adultery" (Matthew 19:9). "You shall not commit adultery" (Matthew 19:18). "...adulteries, fornications...All these evil things come from within and defile a man" (Mark 7:21,23). "Whoever divorces his wife and marries another commits adultery against her. And if a woman divorces her husband and marries another, she commits adultery" (Mark 10:11-12). "Do not commit adultery" (Mark 10:19). "Whoever divorces his wife and marries another commits adultery; and whoever marries her who is divorced from her husband commits adultery" (Luke 16:18). "You know the commandments: Do not commit adultery" (Luke 18:20). "'Teacher, this woman was caught in adultery'...And Jesus said to her...'sin no more'" (John 8:4,11). "Indeed I will cast her into a sickbed, and those who commit adultery with her into great tribulation" (Revelation 2:22).

After Jesus was resurrected, the New Testament taught the seventh commandment:

"being filled with all unrighteousness, sexual immorality" (Romans 1:29). "So then if, while her husband lives, she marries another man, she will be called an adulteress" (Romans 7:3). "You shall not commit adultery" (Romans 13:9). "But now I have written to you not to keep company with anyone named a brother, who is sexually immoral" (1 Corinthians 5:11). "Neither... adulterers, nor homosexuals...will inherit the kingdom of God" (1 Corinthians 6:9-10)."Nor let us commit sexual immorality as some of them did" (1 Corinthians 10:8). "Now the works of the flesh are evident...adultery, fornication" (Galatians 5:19). "For this you know that no fornicator...has any inheritance in the kingdom of Christ and God" (Ephesians 5:5). "the lawless and insubordinate...fornicators...sodomites" (1 Timothy 1:9,10). "fornicators and adulterers God will judge" (Hebrews 13:4). "Do not commit adultery" (James 2:11). "You lust...Adulterers and adulteresses!" (James 4:2,4). "having eyes full of adultery and that cannot cease from sin" (2 Peter 2:14). "the lust of the flesh, the lust of the eyes...is not of the Father but is of the world" (1 John 2:16). "Indeed I will cast her into a sickbed, and those who commit adultery with her into great tribulation" (Revelation 2:22). "And they did not repent of ...their sexual immoralities" (Revelation 9:21). "But the...sexually immoral...shall have their part in the lake that burns with fire and brimstone, which is the second death" (Revelation 21:8). "But outside are...sexually immoral" (Revelation 22:15).

The Bible teaches that sexual immorality is a much greater problem than society normally acts like it is.

The Eighth Commandment

Can you imagine a world in which you never have to worry about anyone stealing anything from you, your family, your business, etc.? A world where no one tries to cheat you?

That is how the world should be.

The eighth commandment, from the Book of Exodus, states:

> [15] "You shall not steal. (Exodus 20:15)

The Bible not only teaches against stealing, notice the following:

> [28] Let him who stole steal no longer, but rather let him labor, working with his hands what is good, that he may have something to give him who has need. (Ephesians 4:28)

Yes, you are to GIVE to others, not just avoiding stealing!

If everyone stole and no one produced, there would be nothing to eat, nothing to wear, etc. Stealing hurts society.

It may be of interest to note that the biblical penalty for stealing was to pay the stolen from 4-5 times as much as the value of what was stolen (cf. Exodus 22:1). And for stealing food, 7 times as much (Proverbs 6:31).

Among other things, this taught people that they would not get rich from stealing and needed to produce their own food.

From a societal perspective, we would almost never need locks or carry keys if people did not steal. Also, if people do not steal, they tend to realize that they need to work to produce what they and their families need.

But there are other ways to steal. Improper representations when buying or selling (false advertising) is wrong (Proverbs 20:10, 14). Not working as one should (cf. Ecclesiastes 9:10; Ephesians 6:5-8; Colossians 3:22-24), is stealing from one's employer and/or society. Employers are also to properly pay their employees (cf. James 5:4-6). The Bible also teaches that one who is too lazy to work is covetous (Proverbs 21:25-26). Covetousness leads to stealing.

Committing adultery is stealing from one's spouse and put's one's spouse at risk of disease. Not praising God as we are told to do (e.g. Psalm 22:23; 113:1; Romans 13:7) would be another form of stealing.

Those truly living as Christians are not scheming to try to figure out how much than can take from others.

Not Tithing is Stealing

Many people do not believe that they steal, yet they do not realize that the Bible teaches that not giving tithes and proper offerings is stealing.

Notice what the prophet Malachi was inspired to write:

> [8] "Will a man rob God? Yet you have robbed Me! But you say, 'In what way have we robbed You?'
>
> In tithes and offerings.
>
> [9] You are cursed with a curse, For you have robbed Me, Even this whole nation. [10] Bring all the tithes into the storehouse, That there may be food in My house, And try Me now in this," Says the Lord of hosts,
>
> "If I will not open for you the windows of heaven And pour out for you such blessing That there will not be room enough to receive it. (Malachi 3:8-10)

Many people will not heed God's admonitions. Most do NOT have the faith to tithe and trust God to bless them (for more on faith, read our free online booklet, *Faith for Those God has Called and Chosen*, which is available at www.cccog.org).

Jesus taught that tithing was still to be done (Matthew 23:23; Luke 11:42). And the Book of Hebrews shows that tithing was changed from the Levites to ministry of the church (Hebrews 7:1-2,8-12).

66

Yes, many reason around this, but those that do are violating the 8th commandment. It takes faith to tithe, not faith to claim it is unnecessary (cf. James 2:14-26).

What About Taxes?

Some people consider that taxes are 'legalized' stealing and should not be paid.

Whether or not they are 'constitutional' can be debated, but taxes are the enforced law of the land of most nations.

Jesus taught that people were to pay taxes:

> [14] When they had come, they said to Him, "Teacher, we know that You are true, and care about no one; for You do not regard the person of men, but teach the way of God in truth. Is it lawful to pay taxes to Caesar, or not? [15] Shall we pay, or shall we not pay?"
>
> But He, knowing their hypocrisy, said to them, "Why do you test Me? Bring Me a denarius that I may see it." [16] So they brought it.
>
> And He said to them, "Whose image and inscription is this?" They said to Him, "Caesar's."
>
> [17] And Jesus answered and said to them, "Render to Caesar the things that are Caesar's, and to God the things that are God's." (Mark 12:14-17)

Thus, not paying legitimately due taxes would be stealing.

While some may argue that Jesus was talking to the Jews, the Apostle Paul also wrote that Christians should pay taxes:

> [1] Let every soul be subject to the governing authorities. For there is no authority except from God, and the authorities that exist are appointed by God. [2] Therefore whoever resists the authority resists the ordinance of God, and those who resist will bring judgment on

themselves. ³ For rulers are not a terror to good works, but to evil. Do you want to be unafraid of the authority? Do what is good, and you will have praise from the same. ⁴ For he is God's minister to you for good. But if you do evil, be afraid; for he does not bear the sword in vain; for he is God's minister, an avenger to execute wrath on him who practices evil. ⁵ Therefore you must be subject, not only because of wrath but also for conscience' sake. ⁶ For because of this **you also pay taxes,** for they are God's ministers attending continually to this very thing. ⁷ Render therefore to all their due: taxes to whom taxes are due, customs to whom customs, fear to whom fear, honor to whom honor. (Romans 13:1-7)

Paul was writing to Christians. Christians should pay taxes.

Eighth Commandment Before Sinai, from Jesus, and After Jesus' Death

The Bible shows the eighth commandment was in place before Mt. Sinai:

"So my righteousness will answer for me ... everyone that is not speckled and spotted among the goats, and brown among the lambs, will be considered stolen, if it is with me" (Genesis 30:33). "'With whomever you find your gods, do not let him live. In the presence of our brethren identify what I have of yours and take it with you.' For Jacob did not know that Rachel had stolen them" (Genesis 31:32). "How then could we steal silver or gold from your lord's house. With whomever of your servants it is found, let him die" (Genesis 44:8-9). "He kills the poor and needy; And in the night he is like a thief" (Job 24:14).

Jesus taught and expanded the eighth commandment:

"For out of the heart proceed evil thoughts...thefts...These are the things which defile a man" (Matthew 15:19-20). "You shall not steal" (Mat 19:18). "It is written, 'My house shall be called a house of prayer', but you have made it a den of thieves" (Matthew 21:13). "...thefts...All these evil things come from within and defile a man" (Mark 7:22-23). "Do not steal" (Mark 10:19). "You know the commandments:... Do not steal" (Luke 18:20).

After Jesus was resurrected, the New Testament taught the eighth commandment:

> "You shall not steal" (Romans 13:9). "nor thieves...will inherit the kingdom of God" (1 Corinthians 6:10). "I have been...in perils of robbers" (2 Corinthians 11:25-26). "Let him who stole, steal no longer" (Ephesians 4:28). "But let none of you suffer as...a thief" (1 Peter 4:15). John seems to have expanded on the theme of this commandment when he wrote, "whoever has this world's goods, and sees his brother in need, and shuts up his heart from him, how does the love of God abide in him" (1 John 3:17). "And they did not repent of ...their thefts" (Revelation 9:21).

Be productive. Do not steal.

The Ninth Commandment

Years ago, a minister gave an assignment about which commandment was the most important.

And while the first commandment is, from a physical perspective this author concluded that if the ninth commandment was obeyed, the world would be a much better and different place.

If people did not lie, the 'justice system' would be overhauled, politicians would have to change mightily, wars could be averted, relationships would be stronger, and less people would get hurt.

Satan is the father of deceit (John 8:44). That, as well as the violation of the first and seventh commandments, is why Christians do not go to fortune tellers, check their horoscopes, or other such things (cf. Leviticus 19:26, 20:6; Deuteronomy 4:19-20; Jeremiah 10:2).

Christians are to worship the "God of truth":

> [4] He is the Rock, His work is perfect; For all His ways are justice, A God of truth and without injustice; Righteous and upright is He. (Deuteronomy 32:4).

It is because of deceit that Satan gets the world to go in the wrong direction:

> [9] So the great dragon was cast out, that serpent of old, called the Devil and Satan, who deceives the whole world (Revelation 12:9).

> [1] And you He made alive, who were dead in trespasses and sins, [2] in which you once walked according to the course of this world, according to the prince of the power of the air, the spirit who now works in the sons of disobedience, [3] among whom also we all once conducted ourselves in the lusts of our flesh, fulfilling the desires of the flesh and of the mind, and were by nature children of wrath, just as the others. (Ephesians 2:1-3)

Satan broadcasts his deceitful attitude in ways that human beings, sadly, tune into. Christians need to resist Satan and draw closer to God (James 4:7-8).

Satan does not obey the ninth commandment and does not want you to either.

The ninth commandment, from the Book of Exodus, states:

> [16] "You shall not bear false witness against your neighbor. (Exodus 20:16)

Some have said the above does not specify lying, but the following does:

> [25] Therefore, putting away lying, "Let each one of you speak truth with his neighbor," for we are members of one another. (Ephesians 4:25)

Yet many who claim Christ seem to condone what they call 'white lies' as well as other forms of false witness. Christians are to TELL THE TRUTH!

If you are going to speak, always tell the truth. The truth and God's word sets Christians apart:

> [16] They are not of the world, just as I am not of the world. [17] Sanctify them by Your truth. Your word is truth. (John 17:16-17)

Keep Your Promises!

Do not overpromise. Jesus taught:

> [33] Again you have heard that it was said to those of old, 'You shall not swear falsely, but shall perform your oaths to the Lord.' [34] But I say to you, do not swear at all: neither by heaven, for it is God's throne; [35] nor by the earth, for it is His footstool; nor by Jerusalem, for it is the city of the great King. [36] Nor shall you swear by your head, because you cannot make one hair white or black. [37] But let your 'Yes' be 'Yes,' and your 'No,' 'No.' For whatever is more than these is from the evil one. (Matthew 5:33-37)

Some people overpromise. Jesus said not to do that. Christians are not to swear oaths as that, as Jesus alluded to, is a form of false witness. While

Christians can confirm/affirm their word is true, they cannot swear that they can make something happen, etc.

It is terrible how easily people these days lie, and how often even Christians do not follow through with their promises!

God's people keep their word, even when it is difficult:

> [1] Who may worship in your sanctuary, Lord? Who may enter your presence on your holy hill? [2] Those who lead blameless lives and do what is right, speaking the truth from sincere hearts.
>
> [3] Those who refuse to gossip or harm their neighbors or speak evil of their friends. [4] Those who despise flagrant sinners, and honor the faithful followers of the Lord, and keep their promises even when it hurts. (Psalm 15:1-4, New Living Translation).

Because the leadership of this author's former church association would not keep various specific promises, even when reminded, it was clear that the . Philadelphia work (Revelation 3:7-13; Hebrews 13:1; Psalm 33:4) could not be led by them. Thus, the *Continuing* Church of God needed to be formed.

Notice also that in Psalm 15 it shows that God's people are to be careful about gossip. We are not to bear false witness against our neighbor, yet gossips often do that. We are to love our neighbor as ourselves (cf. Matthew 19:19).

Two Trees

There were two trees of import in the Garden of Eden: the tree of life and the tree of the knowledge of good and evil (Genesis 2:9).

It is bad to mix good and evil. The Pharisees did it and were repeatedly called hypocrites by Jesus (Matthew 23:13-29). They were teachers that tried to look good to others, but were actually lawless:

> [27] "Woe to you, scribes and Pharisees, hypocrites! For you are like whitewashed tombs which indeed appear beautiful outwardly, but inside are full of dead men's bones and all uncleanness. [28] Even so you

also outwardly appear righteous to men, but inside you are full of hypocrisy and lawlessness. (Matthew 23:27-28)

But this problem was not limited to the Pharisees of old. Notice also:

[18] For the wrath of God is revealed from heaven against all ungodliness and unrighteousness of men, who suppress the truth in unrighteousness, [19] because what may be known of God is manifest in them, for God has shown it to them. (Romans 1:18-19)

Many false religious leaders have read much or all of the Bible, but refuse to teach it properly. Even the two-horned beast of Revelation 13:11-16 will apparently be like that. As prophesied, false teachers have affected many (2 Peter 2:1-3).

Pride

The Bible warns a lot against pride, haughtiness, and hypocrisy. All are basically forms of false witness against oneself and often others.

Lucifer had pride. Eve had pride. It is a lie to trust oneself above God. Vanity is a lie.

But the "pride of life" (1 John 2:16) affects everyone to one degree or another. Pride puffs up (1 Timothy 3:6). Furthermore, consider that "every man at his best state is altogether vanity" (Psalm 39:5, KJV). Vanity is the quality of being worthless or futile. Pride and haughtiness lead to destruction (Proverbs 16:18). Vanity is a common form of false witness.

Trust God and do not lean to prideful wrong understandings (Proverbs 3:5-7).

Ninth Commandment Before Sinai, from Jesus, and After Jesus' Death

The Bible shows the ninth commandment was in place before Mt. Sinai:

"You are of your father the devil, and the desires of your father you want to do. He was a murderer from the beginning, and does not stand in the truth, because there is no truth in him. When he speaks a lie, he speaks from his own resources, for he is a liar and the father of it "

(John 8:44). "Then the serpent said to the woman, "You will not surely die"...The woman said, 'The serpent deceived me, and I ate'. So the LORD God said to the serpent: 'Because you have done this, You are cursed'"(Genesis 3:4,13-14). "But you forgers of lies, You are all worthless physicians" (Job 13:4). "Now if it is not so, who will prove me a liar, And make my speech worth nothing?" (Job 24:25). "My lips will not speak wickedness, nor my tongue utter deceit" (Job 27:4). "Should I lie concerning my right?" (Job 34:6). "For truly my words are not false" (Job 36:4).

Jesus taught and expanded the ninth commandment:

"Again you have heard that it was said to those of old, 'You shall not swear falsely, but shall perform your oaths to the Lord. But I say to you, do not swear at all" (Matthew 5:33-34). "For out of the heart proceed evil thoughts...false witness...These are the things which defile a man" (Matthew 15:19-20). "You shall not bear false witness" (Matthew 19:18). "Do not bear false witness" (Mark 10:19). "You know the commandments:...Do not bear false witness" (Luke 18:20). "And you have tested those who say they are apostles and are not, and have found them liars" (Revelation 2:2).

After Jesus was resurrected, the New Testament taught the ninth commandment:

"You shall not bear false witness" (Romans 13:9). "Therefore, putting away lying" (Ephesians 4:25). "Do not lie to one another" (Colossians 3:9). "the lawless and insubordinate...liars...perjurers" (1 Timothy 1:9,10). "Now the Spirit expressly says that in latter times some will depart from the faith, giving heed to deceiving spirits and doctrines of demons, speaking lies in hypocrisy" (1 Timothy 4:1-2). "But know this, that in the last days perilous times will come: For men will be...slanderers" (2 Timothy 3:1,3). "God, who cannot lie" (Titus 1:2). "it is impossible for God to lie" (Hebrews 6:18). "Ananias, why has Satan filled your heart to lie...You have not lied to men but to God" (Acts 5:3,4). "They also set up false witnesses" (Acts 6:13). "having a good conscience, that when they defame you as evildoers, those who defile your good conduct in Christ may be ashamed" (1 Peter 3:16). "By covetousness they will exploit you with deceptive words; for a long time their judgment has not been idle, and their destruction does not slumber" (2 Peter 2:3). He who says 'I know Him', and does not keep His commandments is a liar, and the truth is not in him" (1 John 2:4). "I have not written to you because you do not know the truth, but because you know it, and that no lie is of the truth" (1 John 2:21). "And you have tested those who say they are apostles and are not, and have found them liars" (Revelation 2:2). "But ...liars...shall have their part in the lake that burns with fire and brimstone, which is the second death" (Rev 21:8). "But outside are...whoever loves and practices a lie" (Revelation 22:15).

The world would be a so much better place if people did not lie and would keep their word.

The Tenth Commandment

Contrary to how the world views it, Jesus said:

> [15] Take heed and beware of covetousness, for one's life does not consist in the abundance of the things he possesses. (Luke 12:15)

Most modern people disagree. There have been articles stating that covetousness is good because it keeps the economy moving and other similar dribble.

Many feel that they need to 'keep up with the Jones' or are otherwise entitled to have more than perhaps they earn. Many go into debt as the covet approval of others and will buy items for show as opposed to need.

Christians should be try to be content. The Apostle Paul who wrote:

> [6] Now godliness with contentment is great gain. [7] For we brought nothing into this world, and it is certain we can carry nothing out. [8] And having food and clothing, with these we shall be content. [9] But those who desire to be rich fall into temptation and a snare, and into many foolish and harmful lusts which drown men in destruction and perdition. (1 Timothy 6:6-9)

Gambling is often a form of covetousness. While 'gaming' can have some entertainment value, most who gamble are coveting what they are not entitled to.

What about lottery tickets?

Overall, lotteries are a 'tax' on the poor as they are the ones most likely to purchase lottery tickets. Many of the poor feel that their circumstances cannot be changed, so they may as well buy lottery tickets and hope that winning will solve their problems. This is a tremendous disincentive to the poor. One should work, tithe, and try to improve one's skills to benefit themselves and others— placing trust in lotteries is not the way people should go.

The tenth commandment, from the Book of Exodus, states:

[17] "You shall not covet your neighbor's house; you shall not covet your neighbor's wife, nor his male servant, nor his female servant, nor his ox, nor his donkey, nor anything that is your neighbor's." (Exodus 20:17)

Satan, War, and a Solution

Satan has used covetousness as a temptation since the time of Eve (Genesis 3:6).

Many problems are because of covetousness:

> [1] Where do wars and fights come from among you? Do they not come from your desires for pleasure that war in your members? [2] You lust and do not have. You murder and covet and cannot obtain. You fight and war. (James 4:1-2)

In the above, James was actually writing about spiritual warfare (cf. James 4:3-6), but covetousness often causes physical wars as well.

James actually gives a way to deal with covetousness and other sins:

> [6] But He gives more grace. Therefore He says:
>
> "God resists the proud, But gives grace to the humble."
>
> [7] Therefore submit to God. Resist the devil and he will flee from you. [8] Draw near to God and He will draw near to you. Cleanse your hands, you sinners; and purify your hearts, you double-minded. [9] Lament and mourn and weep! Let your laughter be turned to mourning and your joy to gloom. [10] Humble yourselves in the sight of the Lord, and He will lift you up. (James 4:6-10)

If you will humble yourself before God and resist the devil, God will lift you up and you will not need to be a slave to sin (John 8:34-36). The devil appeals to pride, covetousness, and self-deceit.

Coveting

Notice something from the Old and New Testaments

> ³¹ Do not look on the wine when it is red, When it sparkles in the cup, When it swirls around smoothly; (Proverbs 23:31)

> ²⁸ But I say to you that whoever looks at a woman to lust for her has already committed adultery with her in his heart. (Matthew 5:28)

Improper desire leads to sin:

> ¹⁴ But each one is tempted when he is drawn away by his own desires and enticed. ¹⁵ Then, when desire has conceived, it gives birth to sin; and sin, when it is full-grown, brings forth death. (James 1:14-15)

Do not dwell on things you should not have. Thus, do not view pornography, horoscopes, or alcohol if you have a problem with it, or anything else you should not have.

The Apostle Paul was inspired to write:

> ¹⁶ Do you not know that you are the temple of God and that the Spirit of God dwells in you? ¹⁷ If anyone defiles the temple of God, God will destroy him. For the temple of God is holy, which temple you are. (1 Corinthians 3:16-17)

Consider that gluttony (Proverbs 23:21), adultery (Proverbs 6:27-29), drunkenness (Ephesians 5:18) and sexual immorality are harmful physically as well as sins against the body (1 Corinthians 6:18). Those who become slaves to lusts of the flesh will not inherit the kingdom of God (Galatians 5:16-21).

Tenth Commandment Before Sinai, from Jesus, and After Jesus' Death

The Bible shows the tenth commandment was in place before Mt. Sinai:

> "So when the woman saw...a tree desirable to make one wise, she took of its fruit and ate" (Genesis 3:6). "Then the LORD saw that the

wickedness of man was great in the earth, and that every intent of the thoughts of his heart was only evil continually" (Genesis 6:5); because this law was in effect God decided to destroy humankind with the flood (Genesis 6:7). "The enemy has said, "My desire (KJV "lust") shall be satisfied on them" (Exodus 15:9). "Moreover you shall select from all the people able men, such as fear God, men of truth, hating covetousness" (Exodus 18:21). "I have made a covenant with my eyes; Why then should I look upon a young woman?" (Job 31:1). "If my heart has been enticed by a woman, or if I have lurked at my neighbors door, then let my wife grind for another, and let others bow down over her. For that would be wickedness; yes it would be deserving of judgement" (Job 31:9-11).

Jesus taught and expanded the tenth commandment:

"Do not worry about your life, what you will eat or what you will drink, nor about your body, what you will put on" (Matthew 6:25). "For out of the heart proceed evil thoughts...These are the things which defile a man" (Matthew 15:19-20). "... covetousness... All these evil things come from within and defile a man" (Mark 7:22-23).

After Jesus was resurrected, the New Testament taught the tenth commandment:

"being filled with all unrighteousness...covetousness" (Romans 1:29). "You shall not covet" (Romans 7:7). "You shall not covet" (Romans 13:9). "But now I have written to you not to keep company with anyone named a brother, who is...covetous" (1 Corinthians 5:11). "nor covetous...will inherit the kingdom of God" (1 Corinthians 6:10). "we should not lust after evil things as they also lusted" (1 Corinthians 10:6). "you shall not fulfill the lust of the flesh" (Galatians 5:16). "For this you know that no fornicator...nor covetous man, who is an idolater, has any inheritance in the kingdom of Christ and God" (Ephesians 5:5). "Therefore put to death...covetousness, which is idolatry" (Colossians 3:5). "For neither at any time did we use flattering words, as you know, nor a cloak for covetousness" (1 Thessalonians 2:5). "Let your conduct be without covetousness; be content with such things as you have" (Hebrews 13:5). "By covetousness they will exploit you with deceptive words; for a long time their judgment has not been idle, and their destruction does not slumber" (2 Peter 2:3). "You lust...and covet" (James 4:2)."They have a heart trained in covetous practices and are accursed children" (2 Peter 2:14). "For all that is in the world--the lust of the flesh, the lust of the eyes, and the pride of life--is not of the Father but is of the world" (1 John 2:16).

Satan thrives on covetousness. Resist the devil and he will flee from you (James 4:7).

Church History and the Ten Commandments

It rarely ceases to amaze this author that people who think that they are Christian do not believe that they actually need to strive to keep the Ten Commandments.

The Apostle Paul kept the Ten Commandments (Acts 21:18-24; 28:17-19) as did the other apostles. There were not true Christians that did not strive to keep them.

Simon Magus and Marcion

The apostate and false apostle Simon Magus (Acts 8:13-23) is believed to have taught against the Ten Commandments (Against Heresies. Book III, Chapter 12, Verses 11-12; cf. Acts 8:23).

A major second century apostate known to have taught against the Ten Commandments and the Sabbath was Marcion of Pontus, who later went to Rome.

Marcion taught "his disciples to believe in some other god greater than the Creator" (Justin. First Apology, Chapter XXVI). Despite being a major apostate, he has been called 'the first Protestant' (Harnack A. Marcion and his impact on church history Volume 150 of Texte und Untersuchungen zur Geschichte der altchristlichen Literature).

It should be noted that there was no faith like the type of Protestantism currently seen in many parts of the world in the beginning of the Christian church (check out also the online booklet, *Continuing History of the Church of God*). All early true Christians believed in keeping the Ten Commandments.

Marcion, himself, was condemned by Church of God Bishop/Pastor Polycarp of Smyrna as "the first-born of Satan" (Against Heresies. Book III, Chapter 3, Verse 4).

Church of God Leaders Taught the Ten Commandments

Polycarp of Smyrna was appointed bishop/pastor by the original apostles

(Against Heresies. Book III, Chapter 3, Verse 4). "Polycarp related all things in harmony with the Scriptures" (Eusebius. The History of the Church. Book V, Chapter XX, verse 5).

Like the Apostle Paul (Acts 17:2; 18:4 see also 13:14,27,42,44), Polycarp's custom was to preach the word of God on the Sabbath (Pionius. Life of Polycarp, Chapter 22). Unlike the Apostle Paul (Acts 21:39), Polycarp was a Gentile.

In his *Letter to the Philippians*, Polycarp repeatedly taught that Christians should keep the commandments (chapters 2,4,5, & 11). He also warned about following the "vanity of many and their false doctrines" (chapter 7), who were following false forms of Christianity.

This is consistent with what the Gentile Ignatius of Antioch wrote as he warned against false Christians that would not respond to the "law of Moses" (Ignatius. Letter to the Smyrnaeans, Chapters IV-V). Let it be understood that Ignatius did NOT replace the Sabbath with Sunday as people who have relied on mistranslations of one of his writings have claimed—the Greek basically teaches that Christians are to keep the Sabbath the way Jesus did, and not follow the way of the Pharisaical (Thiel B. Ignatius and the Sabbath. Sabbath Sentinel, May-June 2016; Thiel B. More on Ignatius and the Sabbath. The Sabbath Sentinel, Volume 70 (2): 15-17, 2017).

Bishop/Pastor Melito of Sardis was also a Gentile. In his *Discourse Which Was in the Presence of Antoninus Caesar.* he taught the commandments and mentioned that it was a sin to break them.

Bishop/Pastor Theophilus of Antioch taught that the seventh-day Sabbath was still in effect (To Autolycus, Book 2, Chapters XI, XII, XIX). Regarding the Ten Commandments, which he called "ten heads," he also wrote:

> Of this great and wonderful law, which tends to all righteousness, the ten heads are such as we have already rehearsed. (To Autolycus, Book III, Chapter IX)

Like Polycarp, Theophilus also denounced the lawless Marcion.

Thus, it should be clear that Church of God leaders, who spoke and wrote in Greek, did not believe that the New Testament somehow did away with the Ten Commandments.

An anonymous 2nd century document that has been called "the oldest complete Christian sermon that has survived" (Holmes M. Apostolic Fathers, p. 102) repeatedly teaches that Christians must keep the commandments to be God's people (2 Clement 3:4, 4:2-5, 6:7, 8:4, 17:3-7).

Other Leaders

Leaders outside the Church of God, that various Greco-Roman-Protestants consider to be saints, also taught the Ten Commandments.

Bishop Irenaeus of Lyon, taught "all ... the words of the Decalogue ... remain permanently with us" and that since Jesus came, they were increased and extended and not abrogated (Against Heresies. Book IV, Chapter 16, Verse 4).

In the early third century, Clement of Alexandria listed most of the Ten Commandments (note, he left out two commandments-- 3. cursing and 9. false witness):

> The first commandment of the Decalogue shows that there is one only Sovereign God...
>
> The second word intimated that men ought not to take and confer the august power of God (which is the name, for this alone were many even yet capable of learning), and transfer His title to things created and vain, which human artificers have made...
>
> And the fourth word is that which intimates that the world was created by God, and that He gave us the seventh day as a rest, on account of the trouble that there is in life. For God is incapable of weariness, and suffering, and want. But we who bear flesh need rest. The seventh day, therefore, is proclaimed a rest...
>
> Now the fifth in order is the command on the honour of father and mother... Then follows the command about murder... This is followed by the command respecting adultery... And after this is the command

respecting theft... And the tenth is the command respecting all lusts (Clement of Alexandria. Stromata, Book VI, Chapter 16).

It should be noted that Clement did not mention coveting your neighbor's wife within the tenth nor did he give any indication that it could be a separate commandment from other lusts. Hence, Clement endorsed the same order of the Ten Commandments that the *Continuing* Church of God still endorses--this is different from the order of the Roman Church which came up with its current order in the fifth century mainly because of the influence of Augustine of Hippo (a man who abandoned the mother of his child and then hoped to marry a ten-year old girl, then did not).

The so-called *Apostolic Constitutions*, written in Syria around 250 A.D. states:

XXXVI. Have before thine eyes the fear of God, and always remember the ten commandments of God,--to love the one and only Lord God with all thy strength; to give no heed to idols, or any other beings, as being lifeless gods, or irrational beings or daemons. Consider the manifold workmanship of God, which received its beginning through Christ. Thou shalt observe the Sabbath, on account of Him who ceased from His work of creation, but ceased not from His work of providence: it is a rest for meditation of the law, not for idleness of the hands (Apostolic Constitutions - Didascalia Apostolorum Book II, Section IV).

Certainly, leaders who professed Christ taught the observance of the Ten Commandments during and after the time of Jesus and Paul.

Despite the views of certain Protestants and the Jehovah's Witnesses, these ancient people who knew Greek did not believe that the Ten Commandments were done away.

There Were Compromisers

Sadly, the influence of Simon Magus, Marcion, and other apostates made some more inclined to compromise on God's law. Imperial edicts against the Jews also persuaded many to compromise on biblical holy days like the Sabbath.

While most think that crosses are a 'Christian' symbol, most people do not realize that the Greek terms translated as 'cross' and 'crucify' in the New Testament come from words meaning 'stake' (*stauros*) and 'impale' (*sustauroo*) and are NOT specific to crosses.

In the early second century, notice the following charge against Christians in the late second/early third century:

> Why have they no altars, no temples, no acknowledged images? (Minucius. The Octavius of Minucius Felix)

No acknowledged images means that symbols like crosses were not considered to be Christian symbols then.

It was not until the advent of the pagan Emperor Constantine that crosses became a widespread symbol for those who claimed to be Christian. Crosses most definitely were NOT part of the original faith. It was because of compromise with Emperor Constantine that other compromises with the Ten Commandments were adopted by many of the Greco-Romans who claimed Christ (note that many items in the catacombs that people have claimed were early crosses, were actually millennial symbols per the Catholic scholar Bagatti' Church of the Circumcision, pp. 298-299).

The warring religion of the sun-god Mithras and its customs and dress, as well as other pagan faiths, also affected many who claimed Christianity.

Those in the true Church of God refused compromises with the pagan religions and have continued to faithfully observe the Ten Commandments throughout the intervening centuries (cf. Dugger AN, Dodd CO. A History of True Religion, 3rd ed. Jerusalem, 1972. Church of God, 7th Day. 1990 reprint, pp. 252-253; 275-277) to this present time.

We in the *Continuing* Church of God are NOT Protestant as our spiritual ancestors formed the original New Testament Church of God in Acts 2 and we advocate keeping the Ten Commandments. More on the history of the true church can be found in the free online booklet, *Continuing History of the Church of God*, at www.ccog.org.

Arguments Against the Ten Commandments?

Although Martin Luther endorsed his idea of the Ten Commandments, various Protestant leaders (as well as the group calling itself Jehovah's Witnesses) have claimed that the Ten Commandments were done away, mainly based upon misunderstanding writings from the Apostle Paul.

The Apostle Peter warned, even in his day, that people were twisting the Apostle's Paul's writings:

> ¹⁴ Therefore, beloved, looking forward to these things, be diligent to be found by Him in peace, without spot and blameless; ¹⁵ and consider that the longsuffering of our Lord is salvation — as also our beloved brother Paul, according to the wisdom given to him, has written to you, ¹⁶ as also in all his epistles, speaking in them of these things, in which are some things hard to understand, which untaught and unstable people twist to their own destruction, as they do also the rest of the Scriptures.
>
> ¹⁷ You therefore, beloved, since you know this beforehand, beware lest you also fall from your own steadfastness, being led away with the error of the wicked; (2 Peter 3:14-17)

Peter was warning that there are those that will be misled by people who claim to believe the Bible. He also warned that true Christians need to be blameless. Those that keep God's commandments are 'blameless' (Philippians 3:6; Job 1:1, 23:12). Those who do not are not.

The twisting of Paul's writings occurs today as many claim that his writings somehow prove that the Ten Commandments are not in effect for Christians.

The basic arguments against the Ten Commandments are that they are burdensome (though the Bible teaches otherwise in 1 John 5:3), they were nailed to the cross, and that Christians are to love which fulfills all the commandments.

Yet, these people which rely on distorted understandings of scriptures that have been normally translated by others fail to consider that the apostles and their early followers did NOT believe that the Ten Commandments were done away. Hence, anyone who tries to tell you the opposite is ignoring the "faith which was once for all delivered to the saints" (Jude 3). The Bible teaches that "saints ... are those who keep the commandments of God and the faith of Jesus" (Revelation 14:12).

Nailed to the Cross?

Some teach that the Ten Commandments have been nailed to the cross:

> The Ten Commandments: Christ Nailed to the Cross (Worley W. The Ten Commandments: Christ Nailed to the Cross. 1959).

> The Ten Commandments were given to the Jews; and when Christ came and died they were all nailed to the cross (Taylor CL. The marked Bible. 1922, p. 53).

> The keeping of the Sabbath as commanded on the tables of stone was nailed to the cross ... The Sabbath of the ten commandments had its mission (Orr C. The Gospel Day: Or, the Light of Christianity. 1904, pp. 336-337).

There is only one scripture that uses the "nailed it to the cross" expression (AV/NKJV/NJB):

> [13] And you, being dead in your trespasses and the uncircumcision of your flesh, He has made alive together with Him, having forgiven you all trespasses, [14] having wiped out the handwriting of requirements that was against us, which was contrary to us. And He has taken it out of the way, having nailed it to the cross. (Colossians 2:13-14)

It was the handwriting of requirements that were "nailed to the cross." Which requirements were wiped out?

It appears that two 'requirements' were wiped out. One would be the requirements of the Levitical priesthood (Hebrews 9:1,6-10).

And why?

⁴ For it is not possible that the blood of bulls and goats could take away sins ... ¹⁰ By that will we have been sanctified through the offering of the body of Jesus once for all. (Hebrews 10:4,10)

The other (which is related) would be the death penalty, as "the wages of sin is death, but the gift of God is eternal life in Christ Jesus our Lord" (Romans 6:23) or other specific ceremonial penalties associated with the Old Testament statutes (such as making a sin offering or washing).

Please understand that the expression "the handwriting of requirements" (*cheirógrafon toís dógmasin*) is a Greek legal expression that signifies **the penalty which a lawbreaker had to pay**--it does not signify the laws that are to be obeyed--only the penalty. It is only through the acceptance of the sacrifice of Jesus Christ that the penalty was wiped out ("the handwriting of requirements"). But only the penalty, not the law!

Even Protestant commentators realize this. Notice what *Matthew Henry's Commentary on the Whole Bible* states about Colossians 2:14:

> Whatever was in force against us is taken out of the way. He has obtained for us a legal discharge from the *hand-writing of ordinances, which was against us* (v. 14), which may be understood,
>
> 1. Of that obligation to punishment in which consists the guilt of sin. The curse of the law is the hand-writing against us, like the hand-writing on Belshazzar's wall. *Cursed is every one who continues not in every thing.* This was a hand-writing which was *against us, and contrary to us*; for it threatened our eternal ruin. This was removed when he redeemed us from the curse of the law, being made a curse for us, Gal 3:13. (Matthew Henry's Commentary on the Whole Bible: New Modern Edition, 1991)

Some will argue that you still cannot keep the Ten Commandments (for "all have sinned"), even if they are all mentioned as being in effect after the crucifixion. Does this mean one should not try?

Furthermore, let's look at another translation:

14 having canceled out the certificate of debt consisting of decrees against us, which was hostile to us; and He has taken it out of the way, having nailed it to the cross (Colossians 2:14, NASB)

The *handwriting of requirements* (often also called the *hand-writing of ordinances)* or *certificate of debt* was wiped away and nailed to the cross.

16 This is the covenant that I will make with them after those days, says the LORD: I will put my laws into their hearts, and in their minds I will write them. (Hebrews 10:16).

God's laws should be a way of life written on our hearts.

If Christians were not to keep the Ten Commandments, the Apostle Paul would not, for example, have been inspired to write the following:

11 But now I have written to you not to keep company with anyone named a brother, who is sexually immoral, or covetous, or an idolater, or a reviler, or a drunkard, or an extortioner — not even to eat with such a person. (1 Corinthians 5:11)

9 Do you not know that the unrighteous will not inherit the kingdom of God? Do not be deceived. Neither fornicators, nor idolaters, nor adulterers, nor homosexuals, nor sodomites, 10 nor thieves, nor covetous, nor drunkards, nor revilers, nor extortioners will inherit the kingdom of God. (1 Corinthians 6:9-10)

Christians are to keep the Ten Commandments and not accept someone as a real Christian who does not.

Colossians 2:16-17

Possibly, the most common portion of the Bible that is often cited as "proof" that the Sabbath and the biblical Holy Days are done away is Colossians 2:16-17. So, let's examine one slight mistranslation of it:

16 Let no man therefore judge you in meat, or in drink, or in respect of an holyday, or of the new moon, or of the sabbath days: 17 Which are a shadow of things to come; but the body *is* of Christ (Colossians 2:16-17, KJV).

The above translation is close, however, it added a word "is" (which is why the KJV translators put *is* in *italics*) that is not in the original Greek.

A truly literal translation would leave it out as it is not in there. Notice the *Strong's Concordance* numbers and related words for verse 17:

3739. 2076 4639... 3588... 3195....3588 1161 4983 9999 3588 5547
Which are   a shadow of things to come; the ....but. body .... of.. Christ.

It should be noted that 9999 means that there was no word in the biblical text—the word "is" is not in this scripture.

Because the same three *Strong's* words (#4983, 3588, & 5547) are used four other times in the New Testament and in those times the KJV translates them as "body of Christ" (Romans 7:4; 1 Corinthians 10:16; 1 Corinthians 12:27; Ephesians 4:12)--as does the NKJV—so should have the KJV.

Therefore, if those translators were simply consistent with themselves, they would have translated Colossians 2:16-17 to state (and included parentheses or commas):

> 16 Therefore let no man judge YOU in eating and drinking or in respect of a festival or of an observance of the new moon or of a sabbath 17 (for those things are a shadow of the things to come), but the body of Christ.

Or in other words, do not let those outside the 'body of Christ' (the church, Colossians 1:18) judge you regarding Holy Days, but only the true Church of God itself. Colossians 2:16-17 is not saying that the Sabbath and Holy Days are done away (more on the Holy Days can be found in the online booklet, *Should You Observe God's Holy Days or Demonic Holidays?*).

It is sad that modern translators of the Greek have often ignored what the expression really meant. Christians who lived in the first and second centuries and understood *koine* Greek did NOT believe that the Sabbath was done away!

It is poor exegesis (biblical interpretation) to rely on a mistranslation to claim that the Sabbath and holy days are done away with.

Galatians 4:8-10

Another objection to keeping the Sabbath is Galatians 4:8-10. Some Protestants tend to use this to say that no biblical dates are to be observed. So let's look at what those scriptures actually teach:

> [8] But then, indeed, when you did not know God, you served those which by nature are not gods. [9] But now after you have known God, or rather are known by God, how is it that you turn again to the weak and beggarly elements, to which you desire again to be in bondage? 10 You observe days and months and seasons and years.

There are several problems with the anti-Holy Day argument here.

One is that the Galatians were Gentiles (although there were apparently some Jews addressed in later verses) and were NOT keeping the biblical Holy Days or Sabbath prior to conversion.

Plus, there is no way that the Bible would call biblical requirements as "beggarly elements." Paul was clearly warning against pagan observances as the Galatians had "served those which by nature were not gods."

Another is that Catholics/Protestants/Eastern Orthodox should consider that they often do observe various days and years (Sunday, Easter, Christmas, New Year's), so they should not observe anything if they feel that no religious days are to be observed.

Galatians 4:8-10 is not doing away with the biblical Holy Days, but instead is a warning against clinging to non-biblical observances.

More Verses

There are other verses some point to as 'proof' that Christians do not need to keep the Ten Commandments that we will look at.

Notice the following:

⁴ And we have such trust through Christ toward God. ⁵ Not that we are sufficient of ourselves to think of anything as being from ourselves, but our sufficiency is from God, ⁶ who also made us sufficient as ministers of the new covenant, not of the letter but of the Spirit; for the letter kills, but the Spirit gives life. ⁷ But if the ministry of death, written and engraved on stones, was glorious, so that the children of Israel could not look steadily at the face of Moses because of the glory of his countenance, which glory was passing away, ⁸ how will the ministry of the Spirit not be more glorious? ⁹ For if the ministry of condemnation had glory, the ministry of righteousness exceeds much more in glory. (2 Corinthians 3:4-9)

Someone referring to that wrote:

Reference is made here to a code that was "engraved in letters in stones" and it is said that "the sons of Israel could not gaze intently at the face of Moses" on the occasion when it was delivered to them. What is this describing? Exodus 34:1 shows that it is the giving of the Ten Commandments; these were the commandments engraved on stone. Obviously these are included in what the scripture here says "was to be done away with."

Two points: First, there was a change from the Levitical ministry and its animal sacrifices. Second, the ministry of death included the written death penalty, which was NOT listed on the tablets engraved with the Ten Commandments. The administration of death was inscribed on large stones after crossing the Jordan (Deuteronomy 27:2-8). As far as engraving or inscribing the laws, commandments, statutes, and judgments goes (Deuteronomy 26:16-18), this was basically done on large stones that had a type of white plaster on them (cf. Deuteronomy 27:2, KJV).

In the Church of God, we do not administer the death penalty to people nor sacrifice animals for sin. Christians are supposed to forgive men of their trespasses (Matthew 6:14-15). We are not to take revenge (Romans 12:19), but are to rely on God to deal with those who violate His laws or harm us (Romans 12:18-21).

Notice the following from the Bible and how someone improperly interprets this:

⁶ But now we have been delivered from the law, having died to what we were held by, so that we should serve in the newness of the Spirit and not in the oldness of the letter. ⁷ What shall we say then? Is the law sin? Certainly not! On the contrary, I would not have known sin except through the law. For I would not have known covetousness unless the law had said, "You shall not covet." ⁸ But sin, taking opportunity by the commandment, produced in me all manner of evil desire. For apart from the law sin was dead. ⁹ I was alive once without the law, but when the commandment came, sin revived and I died. ¹⁰ And the commandment, which was to bring life, I found to bring death. ¹¹ For sin, taking occasion by the commandment, deceived me, and by it killed me. ¹² Therefore the law is holy, and the commandment holy and just and good. (Romans 7:6-12)

Here, immediately after writing that Jewish Christians had been "discharged from the Law," what example from the Law does Paul cite? The Tenth Commandment, thus showing that it was included in the Law from which they had been discharged.

No Christians really feels that Paul was teaching that covetousness was fine for Christians. Paul was saying that Christians are to better serve the law (in the spirit, like Jesus taught with the beatitudes in Matthew 5-6), and that the law defined sins, like covetousness, that he would not naturally have considered to be sin.

Here is a supposed anti-Sabbath verse:

⁵ One person esteems one day above another; another esteems every day alike. Let each be fully convinced in his own mind. (Romans 14:5)

But the above is a reference to personally-chosen fasting days (Romans 14:6) and is not related to the Sabbath—which God said was to be kept.

Notice:

¹¹ Therefore, if perfection were through the Levitical priesthood (for under it the people received the law), what further need was there that another priest should rise according to the order of Melchizedek, and not be called according to the order of Aaron? ¹² For the

priesthood being changed, of necessity there is also a change of the law. (Hebrews 7:11-12)

The Levitical priesthood with its sacrifices and washings are gone (Hebrews 9:6-18). But not the Ten Commandments.

Strangely, the following was actually sent to this author as supposed "proof" that the Ten Commandments were done away:

> [8] Owe no one anything except to love one another, for he who loves another has fulfilled the law. [9] For the commandments, "You shall not commit adultery," "You shall not murder," "You shall not steal," "You shall not bear false witness," "You shall not covet," and if there is any other commandment, are all summed up in this saying, namely, "You shall love your neighbor as yourself." [10] Love does no harm to a neighbor; therefore love is the fulfillment of the law. (Romans 13:8-10)

The above says that the Ten Commandments show love, not that they are not in place. One does not fulfill the law of love by murdering, committing adultery, stealing, bearing false witness, and coveting.

While the above only had the last five commandments, consider the following:

> [20] If someone says, "I love God," and hates his brother, he is a liar; for he who does not love his brother whom he has seen, how can he love God whom he has not seen? [21] And this commandment we have from Him: that he who loves God must love his brother also. (1 John 4:20-21)

We show love towards God by keeping the first five commandments as well.

Oddly, after bringing up many of these 'objection to the Ten Commandments scriptures,' which I addressed, a Jehovah's Witness supporter said that the other commandments were in force, but he would not keep the Sabbath command. Many Protestants make similar statements.

But that is contrary to the practices of Jesus and the Apostles, including Paul.

The Psalms Teach that the Commandments Are Truth

The Bible makes it clear that the law of God and the commandments of God are truth and righteous, and are tied to salvation, but that the wicked are far from God's law.

Notice several verses from Psalm 119, written by David:

[10] With my whole heart I have sought You; Oh, let me not wander from Your commandments!

[101] I have restrained my feet from every **evil** way, That I may keep Your word.

[126] It is time for You to act, O LORD, For they have regarded Your law as void. [127] Therefore I **love** Your commandments More than gold, yes, than fine gold!

[142] Your righteousness is an everlasting righteousness, And **Your law is truth**.

[144] The righteousness of Your testimonies is everlasting; Give me understanding, and I shall live.

[150] They draw near who follow after wickedness; They are far from Your law.

[151] You are near, O LORD, And all Your commandments are truth.

[152] Concerning Your testimonies, I have known of old that You have founded them forever.

[155] Salvation is far from the wicked, For they do not seek Your statutes.

[160] **The entirety of Your word is truth**, And every one of Your righteous judgments endures forever.

[163] I hate and abhor lying, But I **love** Your law.

[165] Great peace have those who **love** Your law

[166] LORD, **I hope for Your salvation, And I do Your commandments**.

[172] My tongue shall speak of Your word, For all Your commandments are righteousness.

In Acts 13:22, David was praised as a man after God's own heart (Acts 13:22). David kept and promoted God's commandments.

Love is NOT just a feeling. Love is showing outgoing concern for others. The Ten Commandments help us know right from wrong.

While the basic Church of God view is that the commandments show love, the basic Protestant view (followers of William Tyndale notwithstanding) seems to be that the law contained in the ten commandments is done away and that they (most Protestants) show love apart from the law.

David, a man after God's own heart (1 Samuel 13:14), wrote:

> [8] I delight to do Your will, O my God, And Your law is within my heart. (Psalms 40:8)

God's law is not within our hearts if we are not striving to obey.

The Bible teaches that Jesus was without sin (Hebrews 4:15). Certain Protestants feel that since they cannot do that, they are relying on Jesus when they do not even try to keep God's commandments—that is lawlessness. In the Church of God, we believe we are to imitate Jesus (1 Corinthians 11:1) and strive for perfection as He taught (Matthew 5:48)—this is NOT salvation by works, but understanding the wisdom of God's plan and the value of His laws.

In the view of the Church of God, the cause of many of the problems people now experience is because they have rejected God's governance over their lives, including keeping His laws.

The main Protestant view seems to be that most of the problems people have are because they live on the Earth, and that for some reason other than obeying God's commandments, paradise--which they define as being in heaven--will be better than Earth.

But it is the obedience to the loving laws of God that will be paradise. It is not floating away on some cloud. All will be able to see that in the millennium (Revelation 20:4-6; Isaiah 2:2-4; Micah 4:1-4).

God's Commandments are Important and Holy

Keeping God's commandments is important:

¹³ Let us hear the conclusion of the whole matter: Fear God, and keep his commandments: for this is the whole duty of man. (Ecclesiastes 12:13, KJV)

Keeping the commandments should be done by all people! Not just ancient Jews.

After seeing certain of the arguments against the Ten Commandments, what tends to happen is that some of those arguing against them tend to feel that nine are still in effect (though they do not normally keep those properly) and that the Sabbath commandment is either done away or has somehow been changed.

Because of that, the chapter on the Sabbath commandment was longer than the others. The bottom line is that the New Testament does enjoin the seventh-day Sabbath and it was not 'nailed to the cross' and never shown again after Jesus' execution to be in force.

Some have argued that because of the council in Acts chapter 15, that God's laws are done away. Yet, that council was mainly convened to deal with circumcision and other physical matters.

The Apostle Paul, who attended that council, did not believe that the Ten Commandments were done away by it as he was inspire to write:

> ¹⁹ Circumcision is nothing and uncircumcision is nothing, but keeping the commandments of God is what matters. (1 Corinthians 7:19)

> ¹⁹ Now the works of the flesh are evident, which are: adultery, fornication, uncleanness, lewdness, ²⁰ idolatry, sorcery, hatred, contentions, jealousies, outbursts of wrath, selfish ambitions, dissensions, heresies, ²¹ envy, murders, drunkenness, revelries, and the like; of which I tell you beforehand, just as I also told you in time past, that those who practice such things will not inherit the kingdom of God. (Galatians 5:19-21)

In the Book of Genesis, Abraham declared:

... Shall not the Judge of all the earth do right? (Genesis 18:25)

Christians are to be holy:

> [13] Therefore gird up the loins of your mind, be sober, and rest your hope fully upon the grace that is to be brought to you at the revelation of Jesus Christ; [14] as obedient children, not conforming yourselves to the former lusts, as in your ignorance; [15] but as He who called you is holy, you also be holy in all your conduct, [16] because it is written, "Be holy, for I am holy." (1 Peter 1:13-16)

Christians are to keep God's holy law.

The Apostle Paul wrote:

> [12] Therefore the law is holy, and the commandment holy and just and good. (Romans 7:12)

Does that not suggest that God would have revealed His commandments to humans from the beginning?

Yet, some, in their effort to justify not observing the Ten Commandments, have argued that the Ten Commandments were not enjoined in the Bible prior to Mount Sinai (Exodus 20:2-17).

However, as this booklet has documented, this is not biblically correct. The commandments are holy and good.

> [8] He has shown you, O man, what is good; And what does the Lord require of you But to do justly, To love mercy, And to walk humbly with your God? (Micah 6:8, KJV)

Do not let pride or lust get in the way of keeping all of the Ten Commandments.

The Apostle Paul taught:

> [5] Let this mind be in you which was also in Christ Jesus, (Philippians 2:5).

Consider also that Jesus said:

> [10] I have kept My Father's commandments. (John 15:10).

As documented in this booklet, it is clear that Jesus taught every one of the Ten Commandments. Plus, He also kept them. We are to have His mind.

Is it Pharisaical to Keep the Ten Commandments?

Some claim that it is 'pharisaical' to keep the Ten Commandments and that is supposedly why Jesus condemned them.

Yet, the Pharisees were condemned for their hypocrisy and because they did not properly keep the Ten Commandments (cf. Matthew 15:3-9; 23:13-29).

Notice how the Pharisees seemed to violate each of the ten commandments:

1. "But the Pharisees and lawyers rejected the will of God for themselves" (Luke 7:30), which is a violation of the first commandment.
2. They considered gold more important than the temple which seems to be a violation of the second commandment (Matthew 23:16).
3. "Then the Pharisees went and plotted how they might entangle Him in His talk. And they sent to Him their disciples with the Herodians, saying, 'Teacher, we know that you are true, and teach the way of God in truth; nor do You care about anyone for You regard not the person of men" (Matthew 22:15-16). This is a violation of the third commandment since they were insincerely taking God's name in vain.
4. The Pharisees also plotted to kill Jesus because He healed someone on the Sabbath (Matthew 12:10-14; Mark 3:4-6), not because this act was prohibited in the Law of God (it was not), but because of their traditions. They would not admit that it was lawful to do good on the Sabbath (Mark 3:4; Matthew 12:12-14; Luke 6:9-11), which should be considered as a violation of the fourth commandment.
5. They violated the fifth commandment and justified it through their traditions (Matthew 15:3-6).
6. They also had Jesus killed (John 11:57; 18:3; 19:6) for their envy (Mark 15:9-10), thus they violated the sixth commandment. Plus, they also

apparently plotted to get Stephen improperly condemned (Acts 6:11-13) and thus were partly guilty of his murder.

7. Jesus suggested that some Pharisees committed adultery through divorce (Matthew 19:3-9; Mark 10:2-12), and adultery is a violation of the seventh commandment.

8. Jesus also implied they stole from widows, which is a violation of the eighth commandment (Matthew 23:14).

9. They were insincere, sometimes bearing false witness, "Then the Pharisees went and plotted how they might entangle Him in His talk … But Jesus perceived their wickedness" (Matthew 22:15,18). This a violation of the ninth commandment--if the Pharisees really felt that Jesus was true and taught the true way of God, they would not have plotted to entangle Him. They also apparently set up false witnesses against Stephen (Acts 6:13). They also had part in spreading the lie that Jesus' body was stolen-Matthew 27:62-64; 28:12-13; another violation of the ninth commandment.

10. Jesus said to the Pharisees, "your inward part is full of greed and wickedness" (Luke 11:39), thus the Pharisees violated the tenth commandment (many Pharisees were also lovers of money, cf. Luke 16:14).

Thus, the Bible either states or implies that the Pharisees, one way or the other, violated all ten of the commandments!

Keeping the Commandments Shows Faith

Ezekiel prophesied that the commandments, including the Sabbath, would be kept in the future (Ezekiel 44:24).

Various Protestants, however, claim that teaching the Ten Commandments is teaching salvation by works. That is not the case as we are saved by grace (Ephesians 2:8).

But those who say that they have faith without works are deceiving themselves:

> [22] But be doers of the word, and not hearers only, deceiving yourselves. [23] For if anyone is a hearer of the word and not a doer, he is like a man observing his natural face in a mirror; [24] for he observes

himself, goes away, and immediately forgets what kind of man he was. [25] But he who looks into the perfect law of liberty and continues in it, and is not a forgetful hearer but a doer of the work, this one will be blessed in what he does. (James 1:22-25)

[18] But someone will say, "You have faith, and I have works." Show me your faith without your works, and I will show you my faith by my works. [19] You believe that there is one God. You do well. Even the demons believe — and tremble! [20] But do you want to know, O foolish man, that faith without works is dead? (James 2:18-20)

Jesus said He never knew those that practiced lawlessness (Matthew 7:21-23). Those who do not strive to keep the Ten Commandments are practicing lawlessness, not righteousness.

Both the Old (Deuteronomy 28:1-14; Psalm 112:1) and New Testaments (Revelation 22:14) teach that blessings come to those that keep the commandments.

Do you have faith in the word of God? Most do not.

Even if keeping the commandments seems difficult, we are to offer ourselves as living sacrifices, which is our reasonable service (Romans 12:1), and those that truly have faith will do so. The apostles taught that Christians, including Gentile ones (Romans 15:18), were to be obedient (2 Corinthians 2:9; 1 Peter 1:14).

Those who will not repent of lawlessness will not be in the Kingdom (Matthew 13:41-43).

The 'Mystery of Lawlessness'

Many try to appear to the world to be 'good Christians,' but they practice lawlessness. This has happened throughout the church age.

Notice the following warning from the Apostle Paul:

> [7] For the mystery of lawlessness is already at work; only He who now restrains will do so until He is taken out of the way. [8] And then the lawless one will be revealed, whom the Lord will consume with the breath of His mouth and destroy with the brightness of His coming. [9] The coming of the lawless one is according to the working of Satan, with all power, signs, and lying wonders, [10] and with all unrighteous deception among those who perish, because they did not receive the love of the truth, that they might be saved. [11] And for this reason God will send them strong delusion, that they should believe the lie, [12] that they all may be condemned who did not believe the truth but had pleasure in unrighteousness. (2 Thessalonians 2:7-12)

The above prophecy shows that the mystery of lawlessness was present in the Apostle Paul's day, but that even worse lawlessness would arise later.

Paul wrote that those who will believe the lie from the lawless one (the Beast of the Sea of Revelation 13) are condemned because they "did not believe the truth but had pleasure in unrighteousness." Since all of God's commandments are righteousness (Psalm 119:172), these are those who are not keeping the commandments of God.

The Apostle Paul reported that the "mystery of lawlessness" had already begun in his day (2 Thessalonians 2:7) and that people should not be deceived "with empty words" to get them to disobey (Ephesians 5:6). That "mystery" is manifested by the Greco-Roman-Protestants when it comes to many aspects of God's laws, like the Ten Commandments (they reason around them).

The true Church of God upholds God's law (1 John 5:1-3). It teaches that God set in motion laws, that if obeyed, would bring humanity much good, including abundant well-being and a productive full life.

The true Church of God proclaims that God's law is not done away, but has been "exalted" and made "honorable" (Isaiah 42:21) and expanded by Jesus Christ (Matthew 5:17-48).

Yet, many who profess Christ want to believe the lie that the Ten Commandments are done away and/or do not mean what they say because of false traditions of men as well as wrong translations. Those who love the truth will not rely on those lies, but what the word of God really teaches.

The true Church of God teaches what the Bible teaches:

> [105] Your word is a lamp to my feet And a light to my path. (Psalms 119:105)

> [172] My tongue shall speak of Your word, For all Your commandments are righteousness. (Psalm 119:172)

The true church teaches that God's Ten Commandment law is one of His greatest gifts to mankind and that His commandments are righteousness. Keeping them reflects love. "Now the purpose of the commandment is love" (1 Timothy 1:5).

Well, recall that Adam and Eve sinned when they took of the tree of the knowledge of good and evil. Thus, not all that they learned was evil, but also some good.

Today, the world's churches appear to do some good. Many have given their lives to promote what they felt was right. Many have tried to serve others. Often the clergy makes statements that are good or at least seem good.

That is part of why this is the MYSTERY of iniquity. If it was always clearly bad, people would tend to recognize that. But when good and bad are mixed together, this is harder for most to see.

Some believe that casting out demons, speaking in tongues, apparitions, various wondrous signs are the proof a church is true. But that is NOT what Jesus taught:

> [21] "Not everyone who says to Me, 'Lord, Lord,' shall enter the kingdom of heaven, but he who does the will of My Father in heaven. [22] Many

103

will say to Me in that day, 'Lord, Lord, have we not prophesied in Your name, cast out demons in Your name, and done many wonders in Your name?' [23] And then I will declare to them, 'I never knew you; depart from Me, you who practice lawlessness!' (Matthew 7:21-23)

Notice that despite the claims of mainly Protestants, simply calling Jesus 'Lord' is not sufficient. The word translated as lawlessness is the same word *anomia* that this article has been pointing to. Notice that God rebukes those that err from His commandments:

> [21] Thou hast rebuked the proud that are cursed, which do err from thy commandments. (Psalm 119:21, KJV)

Notice something that Jesus warned about:

> [12] And because lawlessness will abound, the love of many will grow cold. [13] But he who endures to the end shall be saved. [14] And this gospel of the kingdom will be preached in all the world as a witness to all the nations, and then the end will come. (Matthew 24:12-14)

Notice that lawlessness, from the Greek word *anomian*, will abound in the time of the end. The love of many waxing cold seems to be a reference to the Laodiceans--they tend to think because they keep the law and society is going further away from it, that they are fine--but they are not according to Jesus (Revelation 3:14-18). The Laodiceans are not truly supporting getting the witness of the gospel of the kingdom out--their hearts are really not in it--they are not opposed to it, but are not hot (they are lukewarm) about it.

Very few moderns understand the mystery of lawlessness, though a thorough search of scriptures (Isaiah 28:10-13) will help explain it (cf. 2 Timothy 3:16-17).

The "mystery of lawlessness" is related to professing Christians who believe that they do not need to keep God's Ten Commandment law, etc. and/or there are so many acceptable exceptions to it and/or there are acceptable forms of penance to break God's law, so while they think that have a form of God's law, they are not keeping a form of Christianity that Jesus or His apostles would recognize as legitimate.

Many of the Greco-Romans are like the Pharisees who violated God's commandments, but claimed their traditions made this acceptable—Jesus denounced that approach (Matthew 15:3-9)! Isaiah also warned that people claiming to be God's would rebel against His law (Isaiah 30:9). This is something we, sadly, see to this day.

This "mystery of lawlessness" was "already at work" (2 Thessalonians 2:7) when the apostles were alive. This is also related to something that the Bible warns against in the end times that is called "Mystery, Babylon the Great" (Revelation 17:3-5).

It is a mystery to the Greco-Roman Protestants because they normally officially do not believe that they need to keep the law. Many Protestants tend to claim Jesus 'fulfilled the law' and 'nailed it to the cross.'

Protestants tend to believe that if they 'love Jesus' that is how they are keeping the law. But those that believe that have deceived themselves:

> [3] Now by this we know that we know Him, if we keep His commandments. [4] He who says, "I know Him," and does not keep His commandments, is a liar, and the truth is not in him. [5] But whoever keeps His word, truly the love of God is perfected in him. By this we know that we are in Him. [6] He who says he abides in Him ought himself also to walk just as He walked. (1 John 2:3-6)

Lawlessness is a mystery to nearly all who consider themselves Protestant. Also, since many Protestants have historically believed that since a pontiff will be the final Antichrist, the references to the mystery of lawlessness is not something they believe relates to them.

It is a mystery to the Greco-Roman Catholics (the Eastern Orthodox and Roman Catholics) because they officially believe that they actually teach the Ten Commandments, thus they do not believe that they teach lawlessness. Many of them tend to believe that is what the Protestants do, hence they feel that if this reference has to do with Christianity, it relates to Protestantism. They fail to realize that because of their 'traditions' they reason around them, as do Protestants that claim that they keep the Ten Commandments.

The Catholic *Frederick William Faber* (died 1863) taught:

> Protestantism {is} an anticipation of Antichrist (Connor, Edward. Prophecy for Today, 1984, p. 88)

Let's consider some of the Ten Commandments and how the Greco-Roman-Protestants violate them.

There are many ways that the Greco-Roman-Protestants violate the first commandment. The most obvious is that they put traditions of humans above the word of God. They do this in many ways, including the fact that the Greco-Roman-Protestants normally observe re-labeled pagan holidays (Christmas, Easter, Halloween, etc.) as opposed to God's Holy Days. They mix scriptures alongside modified pagan rituals, which most seem to accept.

Ishtar, also known as Easter/Oster/Ostern was the goddess of fertility and war. Ishtar also has ties to the ancient Babylonian mystery religion and Nimrod. She was also called Beltis. Belits was the wife of Bel-Nimrod. She was called "the Queen of Fertility" and also known as "the Great Mother" (similar to how some revere Mary, the mother of Jesus today) and essentially was also Ishtar in the Assyrian triad (Clare IS. Ancient oriental nations, Volume 1 of The Unrivaled History of the World: Containing a Full and Complete Record of the Human Race from the Earliest Historical Period to the Present Time, Embracing a General Survey of the Progress of Mankind in National and Social Life, Civil Government, Religion, Literature, Science and Art. Unrivaled Publishing Co., 1889, pp. 222-223).

As far as the second commandment goes, the Greek/Eastern Orthodox essentially claim that since Jesus came physically, that this commandment is no longer particularly relevant (Ware T. The Orthodox Church. Penguin Books, London, 1997, p. 33), so they now have churches filled with idols and icons. This is despite the Apostle John's warning to keep away from idols (1 John 5:21).

The Roman Catholics have decided that they can combine this command to be part of the first, even though early Christians realized that these were two separate commands.

Now while Protestants do not normally have the same idols and icons, there is some idolatry associated with many Protestant churches (steeples—a sun god

106

symbol, and crosses come to mind). Certain Protestant preachers also seem to make an idol of money.

As far as money goes, the Vatican has vast amounts of gold, silver, jewelry, and 'priceless' art. It also has hungry members around the world, but does not seem to believe that it should sell those artifacts (many of which are idols) to support the hungry. The apostles helped the poor and those affected by famines (cf. James 2:14-17; Galatians 2:10; Acts 11:28-30).

And the third commandment? Consider:

> [5] Then the Pharisees and scribes asked Him, "Why do Your disciples not walk according to the tradition of the elders, but eat bread with unwashed hands?"
>
> [6] He answered and said to them, "Well did Isaiah prophesy of you hypocrites, as it is written:
>
> 'This people honors Me with their lips, But their heart is far from Me. [7] And in vain they worship Me, Teaching as doctrines the commandments of men.'
>
> [8] For laying aside the commandment of God, you hold the tradition of men ..." (Mark 7:5-8)

The Greco-Roman-Protestants often put traditions of humans above the word of God.

Furthermore, despite what Jesus taught about swearing (Matthew 5:33-37), most Greco-Roman-Protestants will swear oaths.

The Greco-Roman-Protestants-Jehovah's Witnesses also do not believe that the fourth commandment is meant to be observed literally. They do not believe it is wrong to work on the Sabbath, plus they usually claim that Sunday is the Sabbath.

The Bible clearly shows that the command to keep the seventh day Sabbath is in the New Testament (Hebrews 4:3-6,9-11). It also teaches that only those who will not observe it because of their disobedience argue otherwise. And that is why Paul observed it.

Even the Greek-speaking Origen understood some of this as he wrote:

> But what is the feast of the Sabbath except that which the apostle speaks, "There remaineth therefore a Sabbatism," that is, the observance of the Sabbath, by the people of God...let us see how the Sabbath ought to be observed by a Christian. On the Sabbath-day all worldly labors ought to be abstained from...give yourselves up to spiritual exercises, repairing to church, attending to sacred reading and instruction...this is the observance of the Christian Sabbath (Translated from Origen's Opera 2, Paris, 1733, in Andrews JN. History of the Sabbath, 3rd edition, 1887).

Origen understood *koine* Greek. Now although many Protestants mistakenly believe that despite what the Bible says, the Sabbath commandment is done away, even Martin Luther, the famous Protestant Reformer, believed that Christians had to keep the Sabbath. But he taught it for the wrong day and wrong number, and wrong way (Luther M. A treatise on Good Works together with the Letter of Dedication, published 1520).

Anyway, another mystery of iniquity is partially keeping Sunday as the Sabbath. Sunday was used to honor the pagan sun gods, and was not kept truly as a Sabbath by the Sunday pagans. Nor do many actually attempt to keep Sunday as a Christian would truly keep the seventh-day Sabbath.

Many think making some effort to keep Sunday fulfills the Sabbath commandment. But that is based on human tradition and outward appearances, not the Bible.

As far as the fifth commandment goes, the Greco-Roman-Protestants do believe they teach that children should honor their parents. But since God is our Father, they will not go far enough to honor Him by obeying His word.

Greco-Roman-Protestants generally condone militaristic murder.

John the Baptist addressed the military this way:

> [14] Likewise the soldiers asked him, saying, "And what shall we do?" So he said to them, "Do not intimidate anyone or accuse falsely, and be content with your wages" (Luke 3:14).

The word translated as 'intimidate' is the Greek word *diaseio* which the KJV translates as violence. *Strong's* translates it to shake thoroughly, to intimidate, to do violence to. It comes from two Greek words 'diagnosis' and 'seio'; *diagnosis* is translated as examination and *seio* as to rock, agitate, to throw in a tremor. There is no way a soldier cannot 'agitate/intimidate' if they are trying to kill someone.

Now Jesus was a Jewish citizen, but His kingdom, His true citizenship, were not of this world--the same reasoning applies to His servants, true Christians, which is why we do not fight. Nor do we encourage violence in sports.

Christians ARE NOT to be of this world! But the mystery of iniquity has persuaded people that this is God's world and that military service is appropriate for Christians.

It should also be noted that real Christians have always been the persecuted, not the persecutors. This differs from the Greco-Roman-Protestants all of whom have engaged in deadly persecutions.

Related to the seventh commandment, Jesus expanded the common definition of adultery and put restrictions on divorce (Matthew 5:27-32).

The Roman Catholics supposedly do not allow divorce, but their annulment and remarriage practices make a mockery of that. That church is in violation of keeping the seventh commandment.

The Protestants do not even pretend to prohibit divorce and remarriage--and that is actually why the Church of England was founded. King Henry the VIII wanted a divorce that the Bishop of Rome would not grant him, so he left that faith and started a new one in his country. And most of the Catholic clergy 'converted' and joined him.

The Greek/Eastern Orthodox church claims to be against divorce, but it allows/encourages priests to put away their wives if they are to become bishops. That is wrong. Consider the following:

> [13] ... You cover the altar of the Lord with tears, With weeping and crying; So He does not regard the offering anymore, Nor receive it with goodwill from your hands.
>
> [14] Yet you say, "For what reason?"

Because the Lord has been witness Between you and the wife of your youth, With whom you have dealt treacherously; Yet she is your companion And your wife by covenant. ¹⁵ But did He not make them one, Having a remnant of the Spirit?

And why one?

He seeks godly offspring. Therefore take heed to your spirit, And let none deal treacherously with the wife of his youth. (Malachi 2:13-15)

The Greek Orthodox priests who drop being married are dealing wrongly with their wives, yet this is officially encouraged.

Related to the eighth commandment, in addition to having a history of stealing land and property from real Christians and others, the Greco-Roman-Protestants generally do not believe in fully tithing.

Jesus taught that tithing should be done (Matthew 23:23; Luke 11:42). In Malachi God says that not tithing is stealing (Malachi 3:8-10).

The 'mystery of iniquity' indicates that since you 'cannot afford' to tithe that you do not have to. This seems good to some.

As far as the ninth commandment, many doctrines of the Greco-Roman-Protestants bear false witness against the Bible.

Satan's tactics include the use of innuendo and name calling. Satan has long gotten people to speak against the true faith:

²² But we desire to hear from you what you think; for concerning this sect, we know that it is spoken against everywhere. (Acts 28:22)

They often claim that those of us in the true Church of God are in a cult. That happened to the Apostle Paul (Acts 24:5,14; 28:22).

Some of the Greco-Roman-Protestants call groups like the *Continuing* Church of God a cult and imply it is outside of genuine Christianity, which is false witness.

The Roman Catholic practice of confession, while appearing pious on its surface, has the tendency to teach people it is okay to lie if pressured as all they have to do is to go to confession and repeat memorized prayers as the penalty to get over it.

While most of the Greco-Roman-Protestant faiths officially oppose covetousness, the reality is that their societies tend not to see this as a problem. They also get involved improperly with worldly politics.

Furthermore, how the Church of Rome handles matters related to death, specifically its doctrine of purgatory, is covetous and seems to be something that Jesus' warned against (Luke 20:46-47). Its early acceptance of Marcion, after he was denounced by Polycarp, because Marcion gave money, has affected it to this day. The Bible warns about a mother church that is too involved with money and political power in Revelation 17.

A Roman Catholic source promoted the "Purgatorian Gospel" as a unique and great teaching of the Church of Rome. It essentially seems to be that it is fine to sin and not truly repent as God will have you suffer enough in Purgatory to earn your salvation. Although promoters of it deny this, that is the end result of their doctrine and that is a false gospel. The "Purgatorian Gospel" promotes iniquity as it does not result in proper repentance for sin in this life--which is something Christians must do (cf. Acts 2:38; Hebrews 12:14-17).

Sadly, the Greco-Roman-Protestant-Jehovah's Witnesses and others have accepted the mystery of lawlessness. Certain Protestants and Jehovah's Witnesses teach against the need for Christians to keep the Ten Commandments. Whereas the Greco-Roman and certain other Protestant churches reason around their observance.

Over time, more and more in the Greco-Roman churches considered exceptions to God's laws as normal and acceptable.

The late Evangelist Dr. Herman Hoeh wrote:

> In Acts 20:29-30, the teacher of the gentiles explains how the apostasy would begin. He gathered the elders (ministers) of the Church at Ephesus to deliver them a final message concerning their responsibility over the local congregations. "For," said Paul, "I know this, that after my departure savage wolves will come in among you, not sparing the flock. Also from among yourselves men will rise up, speaking perverse

things." Why? "To draw away the disciples after themselves." To gain a personal following for themselves. To start new denominations!

Do you catch the full significance of these two verses? The elders or ministers were especially assembled because, immediately after Paul would leave Ephesus, there would come within the local church congregations false ministers, wolves in sheep's clothing, to make a prey of Christians. And even from those elders already in the church congregations some would pervert the doctrine of Jesus to secure a following for themselves.

In instructing the evangelist Timothy, Paul instructed him to "convince, rebuke, exhort, with all longsuffering and teaching. For the time will come when they will not endure sound doctrine, but according to their own desires" — wanting to do what they please — "... they will heap up for themselves teachers" — encourage ministers who will preach what they want to hear — "and they will turn their ears away from the truth, and be turned aside to fables" (II Timothy 4:2-4). This was in the days of the apostles and evangelists. Many who fellowshipped in the local congregations of the early Church, after about two generations, did not endure sound doctrine because they had not really repented and therefore had never received the Holy Spirit. They followed teachers who, for the sake of money, pleased their wishes by preaching fables — the enticing fables of mysticism and sun worship that were engulfing the Roman Empire.

When Paul wrote his second letter to the gentile-born Thessalonians, he instructed them about the "mystery of iniquity" that "doth already work" (II Thessalonians 2:7, AV). Notice: Teachings of lawlessness were at work in Paul's day. The Roman world was filled with mystery religions that stemmed from the old sun worshiping mysteries.

Many of them found that by including the name of Jesus their following increased.

Jude had to include in his letter the admonition that every Christian should "contend earnestly for the faith which was once for all delivered to the saints. For certain men have crept in unnoticed, who long ago were marked out for this condemnation, ungodly men, who turn the grace of our God into licentiousness and deny the only Lord

God and our Lord Jesus Christ.... These are sensual persons, who cause divisions, not having the Spirit" (Jude 3-4, 19). They taught penance, not repentance.

Jude says these preachers separated their followers from the body of believers.

By the time John wrote his epistles, he had this sad note to include about those who at first crept in unnoticed: "They went out from us, but they were not of us; for if they had been of us, they would have continued with us; but they went out that they might be made manifest, that none of them were of us" (I John 2:19). (Hoeh H. Why So Many Denominations. Good News magazine, May 1985)

Do not be deceived by religious leaders that 'look good' to you if they do not endorse, teach, and strive to keep all the Ten Commandments.

The Apostle Paul warned:

> [12] But what I do, I will also continue to do, that I may cut off the opportunity from those who desire an opportunity to be regarded just as we are in the things of which they boast. [13] For such are false apostles, deceitful workers, transforming themselves into apostles of Christ. [14] And no wonder! For Satan himself transforms himself into an angel of light. [15] Therefore it is no great thing if his ministers also transform themselves into ministers of righteousness, whose end will be according to their works. (2 Corinthians 11:12-15)

Paul continued to keep God's laws (Acts 25:8). Jesus did (John 15:10) and Paul taught to imitate him as he imitated Jesus (1 Corinthians 11:1).

The mystery of lawlessness/iniquity is that the religious Greco-Roman-Protestants-Jehovah's Witnesses reason around many of God's laws and commandments, yet still think they are fine.

While many go that way, Jesus warned that would happen (Matthew 7:13). He taught that few (called a "little flock" in Luke 12:32) would go the right way (Matthew 7:14).

The mystery of iniquity is practicing a false religion that looks good to Satan and various others, but not to God.

"God is Spirit, and those who worship Him must worship in spirit and truth" (John 4:24).

The truth is that the Bible teaches that true Christians keep the commandments (Revelation 12:17; 14:12).

The Beast and the Ten Commandments

A major difference between true Christians and others in the end time is that true Christians will be keeping the Ten Commandments.

Jesus disciples asked Him what to expect for the end times (Matthew 24:3). Here is some of what Jesus said to expect:

> [12] And because lawlessness will abound, the love of many will grow cold. [13] But he who endures to the end shall be saved. (Matthew 24:12-13)

Lawless is to abound and less love. Less reverence for God's commandments. Yet, the faithful that endure to the end will be saved. Perseverance produces character and character hope (Romans 5:4). Christians will need hope during the reign of the Beast (Daniel 7:25; Revelation 13:5-7).

Christians Keep the Ten Commandments

The Book of Revelation is clear that real Christians who are keeping God's commandments will be persecuted by those misled by Satan (the dragon) and followers of the Beast:

> [17] And the dragon was enraged with the woman, and he went to make war with the rest of her offspring, who keep the commandments of God and have the testimony of Jesus Christ. (Revelation 12:17)

> [25] He shall speak pompous words against the Most High, Shall persecute the saints of the Most High, And shall intend to change times and law. Then the saints shall be given into his hand For a time and times and half a time. (Daniel 7:25)

Notice also the following:

> [9] Then a third angel followed them, saying with a loud voice, "If anyone worships the beast and his image, and receives his mark on his forehead or on his hand, [10] he himself shall also drink of the wine of the wrath of God, which is poured out full strength into the cup of His

indignation. He shall be tormented with fire and brimstone in the presence of the holy angels and in the presence of the Lamb. [11] And the smoke of their torment ascends forever and ever; and they have no rest day or night, who worship the beast and his image, and whoever receives the mark of his name."

[12] Here is the patience of the saints; here are those who keep the commandments of God and the faith of Jesus.

[13] Then I heard a voice from heaven saying to me, "Write: 'Blessed are the dead who die in the Lord from now on.'"

"Yes," says the Spirit, "that they may rest from their labors, and their works follow them." (Revelation 14:9-13)

End time Christians keep the Ten Commandments. These are not just "believing Jews" like some Protestants have claimed.

With the Beast power, we see someone who opposes those who keep the Ten Commandments.

The Beast Power Pushes Commandment Breaking

The man of sin will promote sin. He is involved with the 'mystery of lawlessness' also called the 'mystery of iniquity' because he will feign being religious and moral. People who have not accepted the true faith, will follow him. He will not tolerate those who actually keep God's Ten Commandments.

The Bible provides support that the Beast power will violate each one of the ten commandments. This power will put himself above all gods.

As far as the first commandment, notice the following:

[36] "Then the king shall do according to his own will: he shall exalt and magnify himself above every god, shall speak blasphemies against the God of gods, and shall prosper till the wrath has been accomplished; for what has been determined shall be done. [37] He shall regard neither the God of his fathers nor the desire of women, nor regard any god; for he shall exalt himself above them all. (Daniel 11:36-37)

116

The king above is the King of the North, who is called the Beast "of the sea" in Revelation 13:1 and the "first beast" in Revelation 13:12.

The Antichrist is the second "beast," and is the beast "of the earth" (Revelation 13:11). The final Antichrist will be supporting the first Beast, and will try to force people against keeping the first commandment:

> [12] And he exercises all the authority of the first beast in his presence, and causes the earth and those who dwell in it to worship the first beast, whose deadly wound was healed. (Revelation 13:12)

As far as the second commandment goes, notice the following the beast will do:

> [38] But in their place he shall honor a god of fortresses; and a god which his fathers did not know he shall honor with gold and silver, with precious stones and pleasant things. (Daniel 11:38)

The Antichrist will try to force people against keeping the second commandment:

> [14] And he deceives those who dwell on the earth by those signs which he was granted to do in the sight of the beast, telling those who dwell on the earth to make an image to the beast who was wounded by the sword and lived. [15] He was granted power to give breath to the image of the beast, that the image of the beast should both speak and cause as many as would not worship the image of the beast to be killed. (Revelation 13:14-15)

Idolatry definitely is a mark of the beast (and the Beast power may use symbols, like crosses, that many will consider acceptable).

As far as the third commandment goes, notice the following:

> [25] He shall speak pompous words against the Most High, (Daniel 7:25)

> ^{36} "Then the king shall do according to his own will: he shall exalt and magnify himself above every god, shall speak blasphemies against the God of gods, (Daniel 11:36)

> ^{5} And he was given a mouth speaking great things and blasphemies, and he was given authority to continue for forty-two months. ^{6} Then he opened his mouth in blasphemy against God, to blaspheme His name, His tabernacle, and those who dwell in heaven. (Revelation 13:5-6)

As far as the fourth commandment goes, notice the following about the beast and the Antichrist:

> ^{25} He ... shall intend to change times and law. (Daniel 7:25)

> ^{16} He causes all, both small and great, rich and poor, free and slave, to receive a mark on their right hand or on their foreheads, ^{17} and that no one may buy or sell except one who has the mark or the name of the beast, or the number of his name. (Revelation 13:16-17)

> ^{11} ... they have no rest day or night, who worship the beast and his image, and whoever receives the mark of his name. (Revelation 14:11)

Perhaps the Beast will modify the calendar and change the days of the week somehow. Various Sabbath-keepers have felt that Sunday-keeping was the 'mark of the beast.' Christians will enter God's rest (Hebrews 4:9-11), the Beast's followers will not.

The 'mark of the beast' involves commandment breaking.

As far as the fifth commandment goes, notice the following:

> ^{37} He shall regard neither the God of his fathers . . . for he shall exalt himself above them all. (Daniel 11:37).

The context of this implies dishonoring his parents, though that is not fully explicit. Consider also that the beast will betray his harlot spiritual mother—and not be repentant:

16 And the ten horns which you saw on the beast, these will hate the harlot, make her desolate and naked, eat her flesh and burn her with fire. 17 For God has put it into their hearts to fulfill His purpose, to be of one mind, and to give their kingdom to the beast, until the words of God are fulfilled. 18 And the woman whom you saw is that great city which reigns over the kings of the earth. (Revelation 17:16-18)

It should be pointed out that since we are to hallow the name of the Father (Matthew 6:9) and the Beast clearly blasphemes Him (Daniel 11:36), the Beast is promoting the violation of the fifth commandment.

As far as the sixth commandment goes, the beast will kill as a persecuting military leader (see also Daniel 7:25):

> 4 So they worshiped the dragon who gave authority to the beast; and they worshiped the beast, saying, "Who is like the beast? Who is able to make war with him?" (Revelation 13:4)

> 7 It was granted to him to make war with the saints and to overcome them. (Revelation 13:7)

The Beast will also cause others to be killed:

> 15 ... the image of the beast should both speak and cause as many as would not worship the image of the beast to be killed. (Revelation 13:15)

> 32 Those who do wickedly against the covenant he shall corrupt with flattery; but the people who know their God shall be strong, and carry out great exploits. 33 And those of the people who understand shall instruct many; yet for many days they shall fall by sword and flame, by captivity and plundering. (Daniel 11:32-33)

As far as the seventh commandment goes, the beast will be among those that commit fornication with Mystery Babylon the Great:

> 1 ..."Come, I will show you the judgment of the great harlot who sits on many waters, 2 with whom the kings of the earth committed

fornication, and the inhabitants of the earth were made drunk with the wine of her fornication."

³ So he carried me away in the Spirit into the wilderness. And I saw a woman sitting on a scarlet beast which was full of names of blasphemy, having seven heads and ten horns. ⁴ The woman was arrayed in purple and scarlet, and adorned with gold and precious stones and pearls, having in her hand a golden cup full of abominations and the filthiness of her fornication. ⁵ And on her forehead a name was written:

MYSTERY, BABYLON THE GREAT, THE MOTHER OF HARLOTS AND OF THE ABOMINATIONS OF THE EARTH. (Revelation 17:1-5)

The Beast will participate in and promote spiritual adultery (cf. James 4:4; Ezekiel 23:37).

As far as the eighth commandment goes, the beast will takeover other countries and take what they have:

³⁹ Thus he shall act against the strongest fortresses with a foreign god, which he shall acknowledge, and advance its glory; and he shall cause them to rule over many, and divide the land for gain.

⁴⁰ "At the time of the end the king of the South shall attack him; and the king of the North shall come against him like a whirlwind, with chariots, horsemen, and with many ships; and he shall enter the countries, overwhelm them, and pass through . . . ⁴³ He shall have power over the treasures of gold and silver, and over all the precious things of Egypt; also the Libyans and Ethiopians shall follow at his heels. (Daniel 11:39-40, 43)

The Beast will take land and precious items.

As far as the ninth commandment goes, the beast will cause deceit to prosper:

²⁵ "Through his cunning He shall cause deceit to prosper under his rule; (Daniel 8:25)

^{23} And after the league is made with him he shall act deceitfully, for he shall come up and become strong with a small number of people. (Daniel 11:23)

People who do not have proper "love of the truth" will believe the lie (2 Thessalonians 2:12). A lie encouraged by 'miracles' (2 Thessalonians 2:8-11; Revelation 13:11-15), economic blackmail (Revelation 13:16-18), and persecution (Daniel 11:31-35; Revelation 13:7).

As far as the tenth commandment goes, notice the following:

^{25} ... He shall even rise against the Prince of princes; But he shall be broken without human means. (Daniel 8:25)

^{24} He shall enter peaceably, even into the richest places of the province; and he shall do what his fathers have not done, nor his forefathers: he shall disperse among them the plunder, spoil, and riches; and he shall devise his plans against the strongholds, but only for a time. (Daniel 11:24)

The Beast is covetous of power and possessions and will devise plans to take what is not his. He even wants God's power.

The Beast will violate all of God's Ten Commandments and expect his followers to do so as well.

Scripture refers to the violation of each of the Ten Commandments as sin. e.g.: 1st 1 Samuel 15:24-25; 2nd Exodus 32:22-30; 3rd Job 2:9-10 (cf. Psalm 39:1); 4th Nehemiah 9:14, 28-29; 5th Luke 15:18 (NIV; cf. 1 Samuel 24:11); 6th Genesis 4:7; 7th Genesis 39:9; 8th Matthew 5:30 (cf. Genesis 31:30,36); 9th Deuteronomy 23:21; 10th Romans 7:17.

Consider also that the Bible calls this commandment breaker "the man of sin ... the son of perdition, who opposes and exalts himself above all that is called God or that is worshiped" (2 Thessalonians 2:3-4).

Perilous Times

The Apostle Paul was inspired to write the following related to the end times:

^{1} But know this, that in the last days perilous times will come: ^{2} For men will be lovers of themselves, lovers of money, boasters, proud, blasphemers, disobedient to parents, unthankful, unholy, ^{3} unloving, unforgiving, slanderers, without self-control, brutal, despisers of good, ^{4} traitors, headstrong, haughty, lovers of pleasure rather than lovers of God, ^{5} having a form of godliness but denying its power. And from such people turn away! ^{6} For of this sort are those who creep into households and make captives of gullible women loaded down with sins, led away by various lusts, ^{7} always learning and never able to come to the knowledge of the truth. (2 Timothy 3:1-7)

While the above includes many, including many politicians, consider how this describes the Beast.

- Lovers of themselves: The Beast will do this (Daniel 11:36). This is in contrast to loving God and neighbor, hence a violation of all the Ten Commandments.
- Lovers of Money: The Beast will steal the "the treasures of gold and silver, and over ... precious things of Egypt" (Daniel 11:43) and more.
- Boasters: The Beast will boast in his arrogance (cf. Daniel 7:25; James 4:16) in violation of the ninth commandment.
- Proud: This violation on the ninth commandment will be a trademark of the Beast (Daniel 11:36)
- Blasphemers: The Bible states that the Beast "shall speak blasphemies against the God of gods" (Daniel 11:36; Revelation 13:6) in violation of the third commandment.
- Disobedient to Parents: This is implied for the Beast in Daniel 11:37.
- Unthankful: The Beast will not be thankful to the true God (cf. Daniel 11:36).
- Unholy: The law and commandments are holy (Romans 7:12), but the Beast will exalt those that forsake the holy covenant (Daniel 11:30).
- Unloving: The Beast is idolatrous, murderous, and a persecutor (Revelation 13) who lacks even certain natural affection (Daniel 11:37).
- Unforgiving: The Bible does not suggest that the Beast will be forgiving (cf. Daniel 11:40; Revelation 13:10).

- Slanderers: The Beast will blaspheme, make outrageous statements of slander (cf. Revelation 13:5-6; 2 Thessalonians 2:10), and lie (cf. Daniel 11:27) in violation of the third and ninth commandments.
- Without Self-Control: The Beast will get enraged (Daniel 11:30), plus exalt himself excessively (Daniel 11:36-37).
- Brutal: The Beast will persecute the saints (Daniel 7:25; Revelation 13:7).
- Despisers of Those that are Good: The Beast will conspire against the people of the holy covenant (Daniel 11:30-32).
- Traitors: The Beast will encourage treachery (Daniel 11:30-32) in violation of the ninth and tenth commandments.
- Headstrong: The Beast will be headstrong (cf. Daniel 11:29-43).
- Haughty: The Beast will be haughty (Daniel 11:36-37; Revelation 13:5-8).
- Lovers of Pleasures more than Lovers of God: The Beast loves himself and what he wants more than God (Daniel 11:36-37) in violation of the first commandment.
- Having a Form of Godliness: The Beast will claim religion (cf. Daniel 11:38) and work with the false prophet (Revelation 16:13-14). But it will be a false idolatrous one (cf. Revelation 13:14-15).
- Denying God's Power: The Beast will deny the true God and be lawless (2 Thessalonians 2:8-10).
- Making Captive the Gullible Through their Lusts: The Beast will employ 'miracles' (2 Thessalonians 2:8-11; Revelation 13:11-15), economic blackmail (Revelation 13:16-18), "pleasure in unrighteousness' (2 Thessalonians 2:12), and persecution (Daniel 11:31-35; Revelation 13:7) to get people to worship him and receive his mark. All of God's commandments are righteousness (Psalm 119:172).
- Never Coming to the Knowledge of the Truth: The Beast will claim various lies as truth, and sadly most will go along with it as they have not received the love of the truth to keep the commandments (2 Thessalonians 2:7-12).

Paul is clearly warning against people in the end who do not show regard towards God's commandments.

And that includes the "man of sin."

Not Done Away

Notice we are held accountable for our actions:

> ¹⁸ As for his father, because he oppressed and offered violence to his brother, and wrought evil in the midst of his people, behold he is dead in his own iniquity. ¹⁹ And you say: Why hath not the son borne the iniquity of his father? Verily, because the son hath wrought judgment and justice, hath kept all my commandments, and done them, living, he shall live. (Ezekiel 18:18-19, DRB)

Breaking God's commandments is iniquity and iniquity is sin. Keeping God's commandments leads to life. That has been so since the beginning. Protestant translations like the NKJV and KJV teach the same thing.

The patience of the saints in the New Testament is that they will keep God's commandments during the time of this Beast (Revelation 14:12).

Some wish to teach that the Ten Commandments are done away. Yet, notice what the last chapter of the last book of the Bible teaches:

> ¹⁴ Blessed are those who do His commandments, that they may have the right to the tree of life, and may enter through the gates into the city. ¹⁵ But outside are dogs and sorcerers and sexually immoral and murderers and idolaters, and whoever loves and practices a lie. (Revelation 22:14-15)

Do not believe a lie! The Ten Commandments are not done away.

Some may point out the Sabbath commandment and that first commandment and some others are missing from Revelation 22.

Yet, the Bible is clear that people will keep the Sabbath and worship God after Jesus returns:

> ²² "For as the new heavens and the new earth Which I will make shall remain before Me," says the Lord, "So shall your descendants and your name remain. ²³ And it shall come to pass That from one New Moon to

another, And from one Sabbath to another, All flesh shall come to worship before Me," says the Lord. (Isaiah 66:22-23)

So, we see that the Sabbath will be kept.

God expects His people to keep the Ten Commandments and His true people have done so throughout the entire church age.

All Have Sinned

Other than Jesus (Hebrews 4:15), the Bible teaches:

[23] ... all have sinned and fall short of the glory of God (Romans 3:23).

Some question that, but the Bible also teaches that Christians sin:

[10] If we say that we have not sinned, we make Him a liar, and His word is not in us. (1 John 1:10)

Since all have sinned, is there hope?

Certainly!

Notice what the Apostle John wrote:

[6] If we say that we have fellowship with Him, and walk in darkness, we lie and do not practice the truth. [7] But if we walk in the light as He is in the light, we have fellowship with one another, and the blood of Jesus Christ His Son cleanses us from all sin.

[8] If we say that we have no sin, we deceive ourselves, and the truth is not in us. [9] If we confess our sins, He is faithful and just to forgive us our sins and to cleanse us from all unrighteousness. (1 John 1:6-9)

Notice what the Apostle Paul wrote:

[24] O wretched man that I am! Who will deliver me from this body of death? [25] I thank God — through Jesus Christ our Lord! (Romans 7:24-25)

¹⁷ But God be thanked that though you were slaves of sin, yet you obeyed from the heart that form of doctrine to which you were delivered. ¹⁸ And having been set free from sin, you became slaves of righteousness. ¹⁹ I speak in human terms because of the weakness of your flesh. For just as you presented your members as slaves of uncleanness, and of lawlessness leading to more lawlessness, so now present your members as slaves of righteousness for holiness. (Romans 6:17-19)

We are not saved by keeping the Ten Commandments:

⁸ For by grace you have been saved through faith, and that not of yourselves; it is the gift of God, ⁹ not of works, lest anyone should boast. ¹⁰ For we are His workmanship, created in Christ Jesus for good works, which God prepared beforehand that we should walk in them. (Ephesians 2:8-10)

Keeping the Ten Commandments is part of the way God wants His true people to walk.

The New Testament and the Ten Commandments

Jesus taught that breaking the commandments was evil (Mark 7:21-23) and keeping them showed love (Matthew 22:37-40). New Testament writers repeatedly pointed to the commandments.

Yet, many who profess Christianity will not truly keep them.

The New Testament teaches that the Ten Commandments show love to God and neighbor (Matthew 22:37-40; James 2:8-12).

The Ten Commandments are not just a bunch of rules, they help show God's people the give way of life, and thus how to live.

The New Testament not only enjoins the Ten Commandments, it expands them. Christians are to persevere and build character (Romans 5:4).

We are not to just not curse, but not call ourselves after God without truly being Christian. We are not just to rest on the Sabbath, but to do good. We are not just to not kill, we are to love our enemies. We are not to just not steal, but are to work and give. We are not to not just not bear false witness, but are to be witnesses to the truth.

We are not just to follow a bunch of rules for ourselves, but we should be nice to people. We should be committed to doing God's work. We should practice kindness (Proverbs 19:22). Pray for others (Matthew 5:44; 1 Thessalonians 5:25). Keeping the commandments as God intended manifests the gifts of the Spirit (Galatians 5:22-23).

The mystery of iniquity involves teachers who claim Jesus, but practice lawlessness. The end time Beast power will be against the true Christians, which are those that keep God's commandments. The commandment-keepers will be resisting the commandment breakers—which is something persecuted true Christians have done throughout history. Though in the end, for many, it will be worse than it ever had been (cf. Daniel 7:25; Matthew 24:21-22; Revelation 13:5-10).

Will you be on the side of God and the Ten Commandments or on the side of the Beast and others who accept and promote lawlessness?

It is only those who keep God's commandments, and not those who believe in lies against them, that will have the right to "the tree of life" (Revelation 22:14-15).

Do not be deceived by false traditions of men—let no one "take your crown" (Revelation 3:11).

Be blessed: keep the Ten Commandments and live as a real Christian (Revelation 14:12, 22:14; Ecclesiastes 12:13).

If you are real Christian, you should "contend earnestly for the faith which was once for all delivered to the saints" (Jude 3).

Stand for the truth and God's loving commandments.

Continuing Church of God

The USA office of the *Continuing* Church of God is located at: 1036 W. Grand Avenue, Grover Beach, California, 93433 USA.

Continuing Church of God (CCOG) Websites

CCOG.ASIA This site has focus on Asia and has various articles in multiple Asian languages, as well as some items in English.

CCOG.IN This site is targeted towards those of Indian heritage. It has materials in English language and various Indian languages.

CCOG.EU This site is targeted toward Europe. It has materials in multiple European languages.

CCOG.NZ This site is targeted towards New Zealand and others with a British-descended background.

CCOG.ORG This is the main website of the *Continuing* Church of God. It serves people on all continents. It contains articles, links, and videos, including weekly and Holy Day sermons.

CCOGAFRICA.ORG This site is targeted towards those in Africa.

CCOGCANADA.CA This site is targeted towards those in Canada.

CDLIDD.ES La Continuación de la Iglesia de Dios. This is the Spanish language website for the *Continuing* Church of God.

PNIND.PH Patuloy na Iglesya ng Diyos. This is the Philippines website with information in English and Tagalog.

News and History Websites

COGWRITER.COM This website is a major proclamation tool and has news, doctrine, historical articles, videos, and prophetic updates.

CHURCHHISTORYBOOK.COM This is an easy to remember website with articles and information on church history.

BIBLENEWSPROPHECY.NET This is an online radio website which covers news and biblical topics.

YouTube Video Channels for Sermons & Sermonettes

BibleNewsProphecy channel. CCOG sermonette videos.

CCOGAfrica channel. CCOG messages in African languages.

CDLIDDSermones channel. CCOG messages in the Spanish language.

ContinuingCOG channel. CCOG video sermons.

Made in the USA
San Bernardino, CA
11 June 2017